Georgetown's NORTH ISLAND

Georgetown's NORTH ISLAND

A HISTORY

ROBERT MCALISTER

THE
History
PRESS

Published by The History Press
Charleston, SC 29403
www.historypress.net

Front cover: Lighthouse photo courtesy of Phil Wilkinson.

First published 2015

Manufactured in the United States

ISBN 978.1.46711.777.7

Library of Congress Control Number: 2015933532

Georgetown's North Island: A History *is dedicated to the protection of the natural environment of South Carolina's barrier islands*

CONTENTS

FOREWORD

As the manager for the last private owner of North Island, Mr. Thomas A. Yawkey, I knew North Island as a wilderness area with no roads, very few trails, one dwelling where a watchman lived and the U.S. Coast Guard barracks at the Georgetown Light on Winyah Bay. The island is the northernmost Sea Island in a chain extending southward down the coasts of South Carolina and Georgia to the St. Marys River, the northern border of Florida. Presently, North Island is managed as a sanctuary, with limited human access, by the South Carolina Department of Natural Resources. It's composed of extensive oceanfront and estuarine beaches, maritime forest, tidal salt marsh and some of the highest dune systems along the South Carolina coast. Part of its uniqueness is that it is one of a diminishing number of uninhabited Sea Islands along the south Atlantic coast of the United States.

Robert McAlister has demonstrated that North Island has a lively history as related to South Carolina's—as well as our nation's—early beginnings. He describes in detail the landing on North Island of the young French nobleman Gilbert du Motier de Lafayette, who became a major general in the American army and played an important role in the American Revolutionary War. Lafayette's heroics in America resulted in many places in the United States being named after him, including Lafayette Village on North Island.

Robert—or Mac, as he is more familiarly known—takes us from the artifacts indicating early Indian occupation to Lucas Vázquez de Allyón's attempted settlement (1526) to the early founding of Georgetown and its establishment as a port of entry. The beginnings of growing rice for export and the shipbuilding industry created a need for safe passage through Winyah Bay for vessels heading to Georgetown. These early pilots were housed on North Island. Ultimately, a need for a lighthouse resulted in a wooden one being built over two hundred years ago. After its destruction during a hurricane in 1806, a masonry replacement was completed in 1812 and still stands today. This lighthouse is the oldest operating lighthouse in South Carolina and one of the oldest in the United States. Mac includes very important details of the early Lewis lamp and the later Fresnel lens manufactured in Paris that were used as lighting systems for the lighthouse. Those lights shone nightly in my bedroom window when I lived across the bay on South Island in the 1960s and '70s.

There is a historic description of life in Lafayette Village, located near the north end of North Island and North Inlet, where plantation residents moved to escape the sweltering summers inland. This account vividly illustrates the differences between the area at that time and its wilderness state of today. There are details about figures like General Peter Horry, Joseph Alston, Benjamin Huger, Theodosia Burr and many others. Today, Lafayette Village undoubtedly would rival resorts farther north on the South Carolina coast if North Island were not so inaccessible. There are accounts of hurricanes that impacted the north-central coast of South Carolina over the past two centuries, especially the hurricane of 1822, which destroyed Lafayette Village. The village was rebuilt during the following few years but experienced its final demise during the hurricane of 1893, at a time when there was no wealth to rebuild. Mac's narrative takes us through nearly three centuries to the present time, when the island has been safely preserved so that it will remain in a natural state. Now its past is also preserved in this history of North Island.

PHIL WILKINSON

ACKNOWLEDGEMENTS

North Island is not easy to explore. Although its history is full of famous persons and notable events from the past, now only a few people have the reasons and skills to access the island. Although North Island Lighthouse is automated and closed to the public, I was permitted to climb to the top and view the same scenes that General Peter Horry saw in 1812. Both Jamie Dozier, project manager of the Tom Yawkey Wildlife Center Heritage Preserve, and United States Coast Guard chief David E. Browne provided valuable information about the lighthouse and North Island. Jamie was very helpful in describing the current activities of the Tom Yawkey Wildlife Center and showing some of South Island to me. Lee G. Brockington, senior interpreter for the Belle W. Baruch Foundation, generously gave of her time to describe the activities of the foundation and show me archaeological finds related to past occupants of the island. Through Lee, I was able to schedule a visit with Dennis Allen, PhD, resident director of the Baruch Marine Field Lab (BMFL), at the impressive research building of the BMFL complex. He described the activities of BMFL research personnel and some of the projects now underway at North Inlet. I also thank Tommy Graham for information about, and a visit to, the Cape Romain lighthouses.

The person who knows more about North Island than anyone else alive is Phil Wilkinson, former manager of the Tom Yawkey Wildlife Center. He knew Tom Yawkey well, personally, and worked with him for several years while living on South Island. Phil and his family camped out on North Island each winter in the 1960s and '70s, and he knows and has photographed every inch of the island, its creeks and its wildlife. I spent many hours with Phil and picked his brain about everything I could think of about North Island. He is also responsible for many of the photographs in the book. The beautiful poem at the end of the story was written by Libby Bernardin.

I also want to thank my wife, Mary, and Cecelia Dailey for reading and editing the manuscript. Thanks to Julie Warren, project manager of the Georgetown County Digital Library, for supplying historic images. Thanks, also, to Chad Rhoad and other personnel of The History Press.

EARLY ATTEMPTS TO SETTLE ON NORTH ISLAND

North Island is a barrier island located at the mouth of Winyah Bay, sixty miles north of Charleston, South Carolina. Its history began after the end of the last ice age, fifteen thousand years ago, when warmer climates began to melt the glaciers and seas rose rapidly. Rising water flooded river valleys, forming bays. Winyah Bay was formed by the waters of four rivers that flowed from hundreds of miles inland. About five thousand years ago, the rise in sea levels slowed, and thin barrier islands of sand were formed at the mouths of bays. Barrier islands grew and stabilized. Yet they still move and change with ocean currents, rising sea levels and the surge of storms. They help to protect the mainland behind them. Winyah Bay has become a shallow and shifting inlet from the Atlantic Ocean between North Island and South Island. The silt-carrying waters of Winyah Bay, eleven miles long and almost one mile wide in places, flow into the Atlantic Ocean from the north and west, fed by the Pee Dee, Black, Waccamaw and Sampit Rivers.

North Island is nine miles long, with gently sloping sandy beaches on its Atlantic Ocean side, a shallow entrance into Winyah Bay on its south side, narrow creeks and wide salt marshes on its west side and a second small inlet from the ocean (North Inlet) at its north end. North Inlet leads into a pristine basin, fed by the Atlantic Ocean and creeks that connect to Winyah Bay. North of North Inlet stretch more beaches along the mainland shore. North Island is less than half a mile wide for most of its length, increasing to almost one mile wide at its south end. Behind the ocean beaches are wind-formed sand dunes and ridges—some more than forty feet high—and maritime forests of

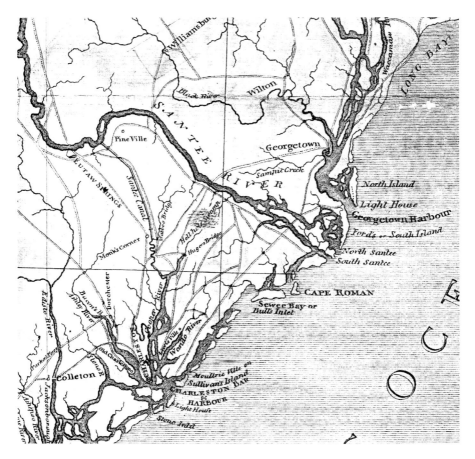

A map of the South Carolina coast, north of Charleston, taken from *A View of South Carolina* (1802), by Governor John Drayton.

pine, cedar, palmetto and live oak, which extend back to the salt marshes. No high land connects North Island to the mainland, a wide peninsula known as Waccamaw Neck, which extends many miles to the north.

The first human inhabitants of North Island were Native Americans, who hunted, fished and visited the island for thousands of years before any Europeans came to America. They traveled to and from the mainland in cypress dugout canoes, which they cut and shaped without metal tools, using fire and scrapes made from animal bones. Small settlements of Waccamaw, Winyah and other tribes of Indians lived on North Island, leaving behind piles of oyster shells and shards of decorated clay pottery. The details of their lives will remain a mystery.

Deer and Native Americans lived together on North Island long before Europeans arrived. *Photograph by Phil Wilkinson.*

Native Americans, dwellers on North Island thousands of years ago, left artifacts of clay and stone. *Collected and photographed by Phil Wilkinson.*

The first attempted European permanent settlement on Waccamaw Neck was in 1526 by a band of Spanish adventurers led by Lucas Vázquez de Allyón. Approximately five hundred Spanish settlers and their Negro slaves landed near North Island and built houses, intending to establish a permanent colony. During that summer, malaria took the lives of many of the Spaniards, including Ayllón. Disease and starvation, strife with local natives and disappointment over not finding gold led the Spaniards to abandon the settlement and return to Hispaniola in early 1527. Records showed that Allyón built a small ship along the shore of Waccamaw Neck to replace his flagship, which was wrecked entering Winyah Bay. The wrecked flagship was carrying many stone amphorae of olive oil, which, if found, would be proof of the settlement.

Later, during the sixteenth and seventeenth centuries, other Spanish, French and English ships stopped briefly along the shore of North Island or sailed into Winyah Bay, but few stayed for long. Some English and French Huguenot settlers traded with Indians for deerskins, which were shipped to Europe. By 1733, when the English colonial town of George Town had been established at the intersection of Winyah Bay and the Sampit River, almost all Native Americans had disappeared from the area, having been enslaved or killed, died of disease or been forced to move farther west by European settlers. Only their names for the rivers and bay remain.

George Town, eleven miles up Winyah Bay from North Island, was declared a port of entry in 1733 and began to thrive as a shipbuilding and trading town. Rice was being grown on the banks of the rivers feeding Winyah Bay and delivered to Charles Town by boat. By 1750, a few men were living on North Island; it was their job to watch for approaching ships and to pilot them across the Winyah Bay bar and up the bay to George Town. In 1762, a Spanish privateer sacked the house of the harbor pilot on North Island and almost carried off a local clergyman, whose name was Offspring Pearce. The December 11, 1762 *Gazette* carried a full account of the episode:

> *On Saturday she (the privateer) chased a schooner belonging to Henry Laurens, Esq.; coming from Winyah, laden with indigo and naval stores, back to the port she came from. Sunday afternoon she (the privateer) was discovered at anchor just without the point of the North Island within Winyah bar, but not suspected to be an enemy. That night, at 11 o'clock, a party of the privateer's crew, guided by Capt. Tucker's fellow, (who was bound) surprised Mr. Bromley at the pilot's house, seized therein Mrs.*

Bromley, a child about two years old, Mr. Joseph Dubourdieu, and several Negroes, and stripped the house of everything of the least value; (the Rev. Mr. Pearce, rector of that parish, who had been in the house some days, having come there from George Town for his health, was happy enough to escape their search; and the Negroes, while the enemy was plundering, all made their escape) they likewise seized a sailing boat of Mr. Dubourdieu's, having stove the sloop's only one in landing, into which they put all their prisoners and plunder, and went down to the point of the island, but the wind being contrary, and a heavy sea, they could not then reach the sloop: After being aboard 15 hours in this boat (Spaniards, prisoners and plunder) without a mouthful of provisions, and scarce any water, she lost her rudder; whereupon the Spaniards determined to, and did, return to Bromley's house, which they pillaged a second time, then seized a large new ship's long-boat that lay there ready rigged, gave Mr. Dubourdieu his own, and went off, but did not get out 'till dark. The next morning (Monday) the boat was seen by Mr. Dubourdieu, from the beach, endeavoring to get to the sloop, which had weighed at 9 o'clock, and was in chase of a ship and a snow that appeared plainly in the offing; as the sloop sailed well, and the wind blew fresh at N.E. Mr. Dubourdieu supposes both the ship and snow to be taken, and he doubts that the privateer's prize-boat got on board; he rather believes she is in some one of the inlets on this side Winyah. The long-boat taken, is London-built, and new, large enough for a ship of 300 tons, was rigged as a sloop, had a truck at her mast-head, and 3 old sails made of osnaburgs. Wednesday afternoon several guns were heard off Winyah bar, whence it was concluded, that the privateer had returned, to look for her boat and the party she had landed to surprise Bromley, who, with his boat, fortunately happened to be up the river. By the questions asked of Mr. Dubourdieu, it seemed to be the intentions of the Spaniards, if they had got Bromley, to have surprised George Town, and pillaged all the plantations along the river, amongst other things, they made earnest inquiries about provision vessels.

A SHORT VISIT BY A CELEBRITY, MARQUIS DE LAFAYETTE

Before the beginning of the Revolutionary War, a few rice planters on Waccamaw Neck began to build and spend summers in wooden houses near the beach on the north end of North Island. Most of the island remained in its natural state. On one late moonlit night in June 1777, at a time of high tide, as her ancestors had done for a thousand years before and her offspring would do for many years to come, a great barnacle-encrusted loggerhead sea turtle crawled out of the sea onto a beach on North Island, laid her eggs in a hole that she had scraped out of the sand, used her flippers to cover the hole with sand and crawled back into the sea. Perhaps a lone panther watched from the top of a sand dune at the edge of the forest. There would be no sounds, save a lap of gentle waves along the sandy shore.

On the afternoon of June 12, 1777, a two-masted, square-rigged sailing vessel furled its sails and anchored south of North Island, at the entrance to Winyah Bay. It showed French colors and the name *La Victoire* at its stern. Its jolly boat was launched, and a crew of ten men rowed north along the deserted shore of North Island, looking for a pilot to guide their ship through the narrow mouth of the bay to safe harbor. Finding no sign of life, they continued rowing in the calm sea, looking ashore occasionally, only to confirm the absence of civilization before resuming their labor. A bald eagle in the top of a dead pine tree might have screeched down at them. It was ten o'clock at night before they reached a narrow inlet at the northern tip of the island. There, by moonlight, they saw four black slaves

A loggerhead sea turtle emerging from the sea. *Photograph by Phil Wilkinson.*

A bald eagle on North Island. *Photograph by Phil Wilkinson.*

A photo of the 1977 Limoges Porcelain commemorative plate depicting the Marquis de Lafayette's landing on North Island on June 13, 1777.

in a large cypress dugout canoe, digging oysters out of a muddy bank. The outgoing tide left their jolly boat mired in mud, and they climbed into the canoe. The slaves rowed them along the shore until a beam of light from their master's house flickered through the tall marsh grasses. It was midnight when the Marquis de Lafayette stumbled ashore on North Island, South Carolina.

"When I felt American soil under my feet for the first time that night," Lafayette wrote later to his wife, "my first words were an oath to conquer or die for America's cause."

GILBERT DU MOTIER DE LAFAYETTE was born in 1757 into a wealthy noble family in the Auvergne region of France, three hundred miles south of Paris. At the age of ten, he was moved into his grandfather's apartments in Luxembourg Palace in Paris and was enrolled in a private school for young nobles. When he was twelve, his grandfather died, and Lafayette inherited a fortune, making him one of the richest aristocrats in France. At the age of seventeen, he entered into an arranged marriage with fourteen-year-old Adrienne de Noailles, a descendent of one of France's most distinguished and influential families. The two families were so noble that their marriage contract was signed by King Louis XV and future kings Louis XVI, Louis XVIII and Charles X. Lafayette and Adrienne were living at Versailles Palace in 1775, when Lafayette, then eighteen years old, first embraced the idea of devoting himself to American independence: "I gave my heart to the Americans and thought of nothing else but raising my banner and adding my colors to theirs."

In 1776, a Connecticut lawyer and merchant, Silas Deane, was sent by Congress to France to seek French aid for American independence. Without Deane's knowledge, a French official, the Comte de Broglie, initiated a plan to have French officers enrolled as officers in the American army who might lead the defeat of Britain without George Washington's help and possibly convert some of the American colonies into French puppet states. Broglie selected a fifty-six-year-old Prussian-born French army major, a giant of man who spoke English, to lead the other selected French officers. This man called himself Baron Johann de Kalb. Actually, he was the son of a peasant and was not a baron. Kalb selected sixteen French officers to accompany him to America. Deane was pleased by offers of assistance from French officers, and he convinced Congress to allow these officers to be enrolled in the American army with inflated ranks and salaries. Kalb was enrolled as a major general. Lafayette knew nothing of any plot, but he had heard that Deane was enrolling French officers in the American army, so he and two of his young friends made a pact to offer their services, writing to Deane:

> On the conditions here explained, I offer myself, and promise to depart when and how Mr. Deane shall judge proper, to serve the United States with all possible zeal, without any pension or particular allowance, reserving to myself the liberty of returning to Europe when my family or my king shall recall me.
>
> Done at Paris this 7th day of December, 1776
>
> The Marquis de la Fayette

Broglie and Kalb, as well as Deane, realized the advantages of having a boy of Lafayette's background as a major general in the American army. Deane and Lafayette signed an agreement, based on Lafayette's "high Birth, his Alliances, the great Dignities which his Family holds at this Court, his considerable Estates in this Realm, his personal merit, his Reputation, his disinterestedness, and above all his Zeal for the Liberty of our Provinces."

Unfortunately, Lafayette's friends saw fit to ask their parents' permission to go to America, exposing Lafayette's intentions and causing an international incident between France and Britain. The French king ruled that Lafayette would not be allowed to go to America to join Washington's army. Lafayette agreed, claiming that he wasn't going to America after all, but in secret he bought the merchant ship *La Victoire* and arranged to meet the ship, along with Kalb and the other officers, in Bordeaux. Lafayette had some second thoughts about leaving behind his seventeen-year-old wife, who was pregnant with their second child. He couldn't tell her that he was going away because he was afraid that Adrienne would tell her parents, who would prevent Lafayette from leaving. In the end, his intentions were exposed, and he and Kalb rode across France to Bordeaux with the king's soldiers in hot pursuit. Lafayette, Kalb and the other officers boarded *La Victoire* and escaped into international waters. The ship stopped one more time in Spain when the quixotic Lafayette had additional second thoughts and resisted pressure from his in-laws and others to abort the journey.

Finally, on April 20, 1777, *La Victoire* got underway for America. On board were Lafayette, Kalb, twelve young French officers and a ship's crew of thirty. It was a rough, exceedingly long voyage of fifty-three days

A portrait of Lafayette at Metz Garrison, circa 1774–75. Artist unknown. *Courtesy of the Lafayette College Art Collection, Easton, Pennsylvania. Stuart W. Jackson gift, 1958.*

to Charles Town. The voyage was a personal horror for the young French knight—his confining quarters, seasickness, bad food, shortages of food and water, fear of privateers and pirates and the never-ending wait for sight of land. During calm stretches of the voyage, Kalb taught Lafayette some words of English, and Lafayette studied military tactics from books he had brought. When the 220-ton, lightly armed *La Victoire* finally approached Charles Town, an American vessel warned the captain that the port of Charles Town was blockaded by British warships. *La Victoire* turned north, passed Cape Romain and the shallow Santee River delta and spotted an opening: the entrance to Winyah Bay.

It was a bizarre combination of men who arrived in America for the first time on June 13, 1777: Major General de Lafayette, who quested for glory and honor by aiding General Washington; Major General de Kalb and twelve other French officers, some of whom had visions of superseding the unsuccessful General Washington and establishing a French military junta; and the crew and miscellaneous passengers and servants of *La Victoire*, whose aim was to unload their cargo in Charles Town and return safely to France as quickly as possible without being captured by British warships.

LAFAYETTE, JOHANN DE KALB and the rest of the crew of the jolly boat followed the black men across the marsh, sloshing toward a light. Dogs sounded a fierce alarm of yelps and barks, and fearing a party of marauders from a British privateer, a harsh voice demanded that the men identify themselves. Kalb, who was the only one who could speak English, answered that they were French officers seeking a pilot for their ship and a place to spend the night. As candlelight blossomed in each window, the doors opened, and Major Benjamin Huger, one of the state's major rice planters, offered what Lafayette described as "a cordial welcome and generous hospitality." It was ironic that his quest for American liberty began when slaves with no liberty led him to the home of a French Huguenot, whose ancestors had been denied religious liberty and expelled from France. Lafayette and his party spent the night at Benjamin Huger's beach home.

"I retired to rest that night," Lafayette recalled,

> *rejoicing that I had at last attained the haven of my dreams and had safely landed in America beyond the reach of my pursuers. The next morning was beautiful. Everything around me was new to me, the room, the bed draped*

in delicate mosquito curtains, the black servants who came to me quietly to ask my commands, the strange new beauty of the landscape outside my windows, the luxuriant vegetation—all combined to produce a magical effect and fill me with indescribable sensations.

The next day, assisted by an American translator, merchant mariner Charles Biddle, who happened to be in Georgetown, Huger told the party that Winyah Bay was too shallow for *La Victoire* and promised to find a pilot to steer the ship to Charles Town the next morning. He urged Lafayette to ride overland to Charles Town to avoid possible capture by the British at sea.

Two days after arriving at North Island, Lafayette, Kalb and a few of the others took Huger's advice and traveled by land. By ferry, they crossed Winyah Bay to the mainland and set out over seventy-five miles of sands, swamps and trackless woods toward Charles Town. They had intended to travel on horseback but couldn't obtain enough horses and had to travel on foot. They soon discovered that they couldn't walk in their heavy riding boots, so having no other shoes, they were forced to walk barefoot in the oppressive heat over burning sand and through dense woods. "Three days later," wrote one of Lafayette's officers, "we arrived looking like beggars and brigands. People mocked us when we said we were French officers here to defend their liberty. Even the large number of French who had preceded us to Charles Town called us adventurers." Meanwhile, with the aid of a pilot, *La Victoire* avoided the British blockade and arrived in Charles Town Harbor the day after Lafayette arrived. Unfortunately, *La Victoire* would strike bottom and sink in Charles Town Harbor several weeks later.

Learning of Lafayette's true identity, Governor John Rutledge, General Moultrie and other leading members of Charles Town's society wined, dined and entertained the group for eight days as they prepared to undertake a long overland carriage and horseback journey to Philadelphia. It was a difficult seven-hundred-mile trek through swamps and over impassible roads, but they arrived in Philadelphia on July 27 "in a more pitiable condition even than when we first came into Charles Town." By the time they reached Philadelphia, Congress and George Washington's generals had tired of Deane's commissioning of high-salaried French officers with no experience and no knowledge of the English language. Congress refused to commission Kalb or his men. Even Lafayette had to plead with Congress and use his Masonic brotherhood influence on John Hancock to receive his commission as a major general in the American army. Congress wrote:

Whereas the Marquis de La Fayette, out of his great zeal to the cause of liberty, in which the United States are engaged, has left his family and connections, and at his own expense come over to offer his services to the United States without pension or particular allowance, and is anxious to risqué his life in our cause—Resolved, That his services be accepted and that in consideration of his zeal, illustrious family and connections he have the rank and commission of Major General in the Army of the United States.

When Congress rejected the commissions of Kalb and the other French officers, their secret plot was dead. Taking pity on his fellow officers, Lafayette agreed to pay their fare and expenses to return to France, just as he had previously paid all of the expenses of the entire expedition. Lafayette selected two of the young French officers as his personal adjutants. As Kalb was preparing to return to France, with Lafayette's help, he received permission to stay in America and was given his commission as a major general.

Lafayette's first major combat duty came during the September 1777 Battle of Brandywine, when he was shot in the leg while helping to organize a retreat. General George Washington requested that doctors take special care of Lafayette, igniting a strong bond between the two that lasted until Washington's death.

Following a winter in Valley Forge with Washington, Lafayette burnished his credentials as an intelligent leader while helping to draw more French resources to the colonial side. In May 1778, he outwitted the British sent to capture him at Bunker Hill, later named Lafayette Hill, and rallied a shaky Continental attack at Monmouth Courthouse to force a stalemate.

Lafayette returned to France in 1779 to press Louis XVI for more aid to the Americans. While there, he and Benjamin Franklin became close friends. Lafayette and Franklin hatched a bold plan to attack the coastline of England, to be led by Lafayette and naval commander John Paul Jones on the *Bonhomme Richard*, but the attack was not approved by the king, so it never took place. In 1779, Lafayette and Adrienne's only son, named George-Washington Lafayette, was born in Paris, the godson of General George Washington. Much later in 1795, while Lafayette was in prison in Austria, Adrienne sent her son to America to live with President Washington's family until he could return to France in 1798.

In 1780, Lafayette returned to America and assumed increased military responsibility. Americans celebrated Lafayette at every turn and referred to him as "Our Marquis." As commander of the Virginia Continental forces in 1781, he helped keep British lieutenant general Lord Cornwallis's army pinned at Yorktown, Virginia, while divisions led by Washington and France's Comte de Rochambeau surrounded the British and forced a surrender in the last battle of the Revolutionary War.

More than four years had passed since Lafayette landed on North Island. Now, at only twenty-four years of age, he had already lived a lifetime of experiences, but he was just getting started. Known as the "Hero of Two Worlds" after returning to France in December 1781, Lafayette rejoined the French army and organized trade agreements with Thomas Jefferson, the American ambassador to France.

With his country on the verge of major political and social upheaval, Lafayette advocated for a governing body representing the three social classes and drafted the Declaration of the Rights of Man. When violence broke out in 1789, he was named commander of the Paris National Guard and tried to calm the chaos of the revolution and achieve a constitutional monarchy. However, Lafayette was obligated to protect the royal family, a position that left him vulnerable to the factions vying for power. He fled the country in 1792 but was captured by Austrian forces and confined in Olmutz Prison.

In November 1794, Francis Huger, the son of South Carolina planter Benjamin Huger, was a student in Austria. He joined in a plot to aid the escape of Lafayette from Olmutz Prison. Lafayette was allowed a carriage ride with a guard every other day. One day, Francis Huger and a friend overpowered the guard and instructed Lafayette to mount one of their two horses and ride to a particular place where a carriage was waiting. However, Lafayette misinterpreted the instructions, went the wrong way and was recaptured. Francis Huger and his companion were also captured and served six months in an Austrian prison. In 1795, Adrienne and her two daughters joined Lafayette in the dismal Olmutz Prison. With help from Napoleon, they were released from prison in 1797, but Lafayette remained in Holland. He wanted badly to immigrate to America with his family but was dissuaded by Washington, Hamilton and others because of the bad relations existing between France and America at that time. Lafayette was allowed to return to France in 1799, when he took up a life as a gentleman farmer at Château Lagrange, far from Paris.

Lafayette maintained a low profile while Napoleon Bonaparte was in power from 1799 until 1813. He vehemently argued for Napoleon's abdication following the defeat at the Battle of Waterloo in July 1815. Lafayette was elected to the Chamber of Deputies in 1818 at the age of sixty-one.

In 1824, Lafayette accepted an invitation from President Monroe to revisit the United States. He made a triumphant visit to each of the twenty-four states during his thirteen-month stay. The people of the United States enthusiastically showed their appreciation for all he had done since his arrival at North Island in 1777. Lafayette visited Charles Town, South Carolina, where he had a reunion with Francis Huger, and he visited Camden, where he set a cornerstone honoring General de Kalb. Lafayette returned to France in 1825.

He died in Paris on May 20, 1834. An American flag flies over his grave. Lafayette's life was never celebrated in France as it was, and is, in the United States. Lafayette's illustrious career in America resulted in many places being named after him, including Lafayette Village on remote North Island, South Carolina.

A SUMMER RESORT
FOR ARISTOCRATS

Between 1777 and 1783, the Revolutionary War had little direct effect on North Island other than restricting the shipping trade in and out of Winyah Bay. North of Charleston, which had been captured by the British, there were only occasional skirmishes between privateers and blockading vessels along the coast. After the signing of the Treaty of Paris in 1783, the governments of the State of South Carolina and the Town of Georgetown, as part of the new United States of America, established commissions to collect customs, build pilot boats, employ pilots, quarantine foreign vessels and provide aids to navigation.

A lighthouse at the south end of North Island had been contemplated for a long time, even before the Revolutionary War. In 1795, Congress appropriated money to build a lighthouse. A contract was signed with a Charleston carpenter in 1798 to erect a lighthouse at the south end of North Island on land that had been given to the United States government by Paul Trapier, the first owner of North Island. The wooden lighthouse was of octagonal shape, twenty-six feet in diameter, placed on a brick foundation. Near the top of the seventy-two-foot-high structure, the diameter had decreased to twelve feet. The outside was covered with rough boards and cypress shingles painted white. Five flights of stairs led past two windows at each landing to the lantern platform. At the top, there was a six-foot-diameter iron lantern room with glass windows resting on a cypress floor covered with flagstones. A balcony three feet wide extended around the lantern room. An oil vault for whale oil, a cistern and a two-

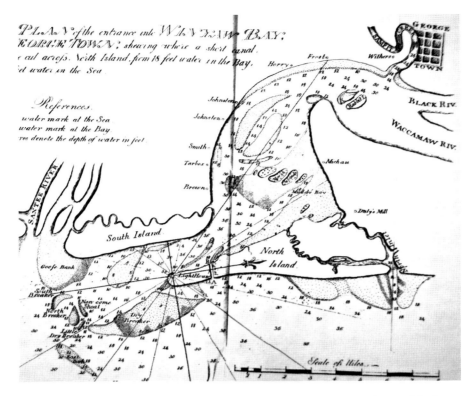

An 1802 chart of North Island and Winyah Bay showing a proposed canal across North Island. Taken from *A View of South Carolina* (1802), by Governor John Drayton.

story keeper's house were built next to the lighthouse. In 1800, a newspaper reported that "the Georgetown lighthouse was erected wherein is shewn a full and brilliant light."

By 1812, there were many more summer residents of North Island than in 1777. Several hundred men, women and children—the majority being black African slaves—lived there each summer. The rice planters and their families along Waccamaw Neck found relief from the summer heat and miasma of their riverside rice plantations by escaping to North Island from May through September. They lived in comfortable wooden houses along the beach and in a village on both sides of North Inlet that was named Lafayette Village.

How did the summer colony on North Island get started? The answer went back several generations to a few early eighteenth-century English and French Huguenot entrepreneurs, including the first Paul Trapier, who took

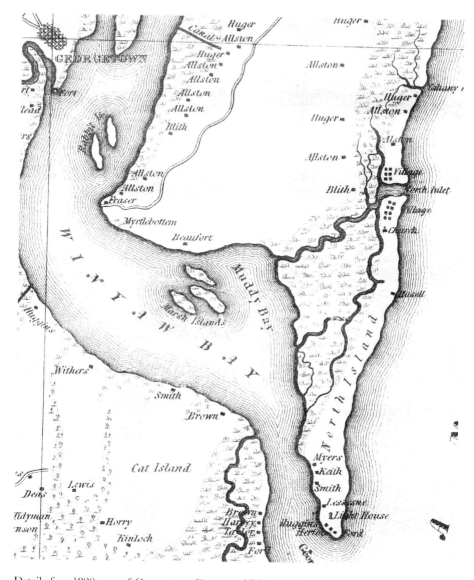

Detail of an 1820 map of Georgetown County published in the 1825 *Mills Atlas of South Carolina* showing Lafayette Village on North Island. *Courtesy of the Georgetown County Digital Library.*

advantage of financial opportunities in the New World by obtaining grants of large tracts of land in Lowcountry Carolina from the Lords Proprietors of England, to whom the king had given control of all land in America between north latitudes thirty-six and thirty-one from the Atlantic to the

Pacific. Divided tracts in Carolina were sold to planters, who settled on their land. The planters imported African slaves from established sugar plantations in the Caribbean and from tribes in West Africa to provide labor for all aspects of their agricultural enterprises. Negroes from West Africa were snatched from their homes by rival tribesmen, who sold them to European slave traders. They were crowded aboard ships and transported to Charles Town, where they were sold to planters. The enslaved natives of West Africa were among the first to grow rice in America. From them, the planters learned many things about rice culture, including tidal irrigation of rice fields, the initial use of mortar and pestle and the making of woven grass baskets. Slaves were assigned the backbreaking tasks of clearing and diking thousands of acres of thickly forested cypress swamps along the banks of rivers, followed by the tasks of planting and harvesting rice. Harvested rice was loaded aboard small schooners and other vessels and transported to Charles Town, where it was husked; cleaned; packed in large barrels, called tierces; and shipped to market. There were lucrative markets for rice in Europe, and profits from the sale of rice were enormous.

The Revolutionary War and its aftermath interrupted the growing of rice for a few years because of the loss of the English market for rice, indigo and naval stores. Rice culture—particularly the growing of rice along the tidal freshwater portions of the Waccamaw and Pee Dee Rivers—recovered during the first part of the nineteenth century. Rice fields continued to be carved out of swamps along these rivers. Richard Porcher describes the difficulties of turning swamps into rice fields in his book, *The Market Preparation of Carolina Rice*:

> *The construction of tidal rice fields was far from easy. The conditions that made tidal floodplains ideal for rice growing were also terrible obstacles to converting those swamps into rice fields. The dark muck soil was unstable. To avoid sinking, one had to step from root to root onto a dubiously stable tussock. Twice a day the land was flooded at high tide. Throughout the swamp, thickets of cat briar impeded progress and tore at flesh and clothing. The heat and humidity in the summer was oppressive; cottonmouths and alligators also must have caught the attention of workers, as well as swarms of mosquitoes. The work went on. African slaves working with oxen, shovels and axes transformed the swamps into the richest agricultural land in the nation, but the "deadly fields" extracted a horrendous cost to life and health.*

Soon after the American Revolution, the rice planters along the rivers had become the landed gentry of the southern United States. Copying a lifestyle of the English rich, the wealthiest of the rice planters lived in splendor along the banks of the Waccamaw River, a few miles above Georgetown. In 1819, President James Monroe visited Arcadia Plantation on the Waccamaw River, home of Benjamin Huger II, a son of the planter who had greeted Lafayette. A red carpet was spread from the barge landing to the front entrance of the house, and upon his departure, he took his leave in "one of the plantation barges, profusely decorated and adorned for the occasion with the United States colors proudly floating at its head. Eight Negro oarsmen dressed in livery propelled the barge."

By the beginning of the nineteenth century, the Waccamaw River rice plantations were among the largest and most profitable plantations in the slaveholding South. A few of the rice planters owned over five hundred slaves, even up to one thousand. These few rice planting families were the elite aristocracy of South Carolina, with town houses in Charleston, European educations for their children and regular trips abroad for vacations. Their lives in big plantation houses along the river, tended by droves of house slaves, were pleasant as long as the weather was cool, but in summer, a hot, humid haze hung over the soggy rice fields; insects invaded the river swamps; and disease sickened and killed some members of the white population. A daughter of one of the rice plantation owners complained about the rice fields during the summer growing season, saying, "The whole atmosphere was polluted by the dreadful smell."

To escape the unpleasantness of summer life on the plantation, many planters temporarily moved away, leaving their white overseers and black drivers and field hands to ready the rice crop for harvest. A few of the wealthiest planters escaped to Europe, Saratoga, Newport or the mountains of North Carolina. Some of the others moved to North Island, taking their possessions, including several of their house slaves, with them to their beach houses. The planters and their families were transported by slave-powered boats, which had been built by skilled slave shipwrights. The planters' houses had been built by slave carpenter craftsmen, who had precut and marked the lumber on the plantation premises, transported it the to the island on flats and erected the dwellings, kitchen buildings, piazzas, stables, sheds and outbuildings along the beach for their masters to catch the ocean breezes. The slaves lived under the main houses in low rooms with dirt floors or in flimsy slave quarters behind their masters' houses.

One of the summer residents of North Island in 1812 was General Peter Horry. Peter Horry, a descendent of French Huguenots, was born in Georgetown in 1743 and grew up on his uncle Elias Horry's plantation on Winyah Bay, Dover, which he eventually inherited. He attended the Winyah Indigo Society School in Georgetown, where he learned to read while fighting a stuttering speech impediment. For a time, he was an apprentice to a Georgetown merchant. In 1775, he was elected a captain in the Second South Carolina Regiment and served under General Francis Marion, the "Swamp Fox," during most of the Revolutionary War. Horry rose in rank to lieutenant colonel, had his horse shot out from under him and received minor wounds on several occasions. For a short time, he was assigned to the staff of Major General Johann de Kalb as an observer, but he returned to Charleston before the Battle of Camden in August 1780, when Kalb was killed. Horry had the reputation for being thin

A portrait of General Peter Horry. *Courtesy of Horry County Museum.*

skinned and not a good natural leader. He had a bitter dispute with another officer over who would receive a command that they both wanted, which resulted in a disruption of plans and a minor American defeat at the Swamp Fox's camp, which caused General Marion to fall out with Horry temporarily. Horry did receive the command to defend the town of Georgetown but was turned down for promotion to brigadier general.

After the war was over in 1781, Horry rebuilt his Dover Plantation and settled down to the life of a rice planter. Soon after, he married Sarah Baxter, who died in 1791.

Horry tried, unsuccessfully, to sell Dover Plantation in 1793. Horry served in the state senate and remained in the state militia. When Francis Marion retired from the state militia in 1794, Horry finally received a general's commission. He ran the state militia until he retired from the military in 1806.

The relationship between Horry and Marion was too close not to overcome their bad feelings, and they reconciled a few months after the end of the war. Marion visited Horry shortly before he died in 1795. General Francis Marion was a hero to Peter Horry, and after the war, Horry began to write a biography of Marion. In 1803, Horry offered his account of Marion's Brigade to the Georgetown Historical Society, which delayed and never printed the account. Horry continued to seek a publisher for his account of the life of Francis Marion. Somehow, he met Mason Locke "Parson" Weems, who had previously published a book he had written about George Washington, in which he had invented the story of Washington chopping down the cherry tree. Without knowing Parson Weems's reputation for making things up, Peter Horry gave his manuscript to him, and in 1807, Horry received the final version of Marion's biography from Weems. After reading Weems's story, Horry wrote, "You have carved and mutilated it with so many erroneous statements that your embellishments, observations and remarks must necessarily be erroneous as proceeding from false grounds. Most certainly, tis not my history but your romance." Later, after Horry died, Weems published his account anyway.

By 1801, Horry owned or leased a summer home on North Island and was involved in the politics of the island. A canal had been proposed across the island, and Horry was not in favor of it. Shippers wanted a deeper shipping channel from the sea into Winyah Bay because the present channel was so shallow and shifty that deep-draft vessels couldn't cross the bar, and several vessels had gone aground and been wrecked. Some of those in charge of the Port of Georgetown proposed to correct the situation by constructing a deep and wide shipping canal across North Island from the ocean into Winyah Bay, believing that it would make for a more dependable route. The chief engineer of South Carolina, Christian Senf, had been consulted and given his opinion that the canal could and should be built. Horry hadn't trusted Senf's opinions since 1800, when Senf, between 1793 and 1800, directed construction of the twenty-five-mile-long, financially disastrous Santee Canal, joining the Santee River to the Cooper River, which had cost three times the budget, taken three years longer to build than estimated and had diverted trade to Charleston that would have otherwise come into Georgetown.

In 1806, after five years of discussions and objections, the North Island Canal was started. Approximately 130 slaves were temporarily hired from their masters by the supervisor of canal construction. The slaves worked like dogs for two years, digging by hand a half-mile-long, six-foot-deep, two-hundred-foot-wide ditch across the island. The work was so difficult that 10 slaves died of exhaustion or cave-ins during the project. When the canal was only about ten days from completion, the ocean broke through during a storm and demolished most of the completed work. Senf hadn't taken into account that the canal's entrance into Winyah Bay was fifteen inches lower than the level of the ocean, so seawater flowed constantly inward, carrying sand, which rapidly filled the canal and rendered it useless. The failed project was abandoned for good—a decision that Horry heartily approved. What was left of the canal soon became a shallow ditch, whose route can be seen as an east–west straight line across the island on aerial photographs of North Island.

By 1812, Horry was a tired old man of almost seventy. He spent most summers on North Island. Horry had married his second wife, Margaret Guignard, in 1793. They had traveled when they first married, but she apparently didn't like life on North Island and spent most of her summers at her family home in Columbia, the city that had replaced Charleston as capital of the state in 1790. Horry still owned his rice plantation, Dover, along the western shore of Winyah Bay but lived in a house in a new section of Georgetown called Browntown when he wasn't living on North Island. He owned about eighty slaves, most of whom lived in cabins at Dover. In the summer, he left his field hands at Dover Plantation under the direction of his overseer and brought four or five house slaves to North Island to tend to his needs. His North Island house was located on the south side of North Inlet, in Lafayette Village, with a view of the ocean. From there, with a glass, he could see ships entering and leaving Winyah Bay and could watch the pilots board ships that were preparing to enter the bay to sail up to Georgetown. It was early during the War of 1812, and Horry often scanned the horizon and worried that distant passing ships might be the British enemy. Peter Horry kept a journal in 1812 in which he recorded the events of each day.

It was June 17, 1812, when Horry left his house at Browntown. In his journal, he wrote:

> *Rose very Early, & all my Servants & Getting Ready for Embarkation & Sent my bedding Chain, bed Benches, boards, etc. with Bread, Rice Buckwit etc. on boards with Some warm Cloaths. Breakfasted Early & all hands on board about 8 Oclock. A Promising Passage (a fine day) Stoped at Dover to take in 2 Oarsmen. Made our Passage from Dover to North Inlet in 3 hours & found my Carpenters forward Repairing my House etc.*

Horry usually arose early to be attended by a slave, whom he would accompany to collect driftwood for firewood or dig sea mud for his garden. Sometimes, he would send his flat to Dover Plantation loaded with what was called sea mud, which was silt from upriver marshes and rivers that had drifted down and been deposited onto the island shores and which contained rich nutrients. When rain had washed the salt away, sea mud was mixed with crushed clam, oyster and conch shells, also brought from the island, and used as fertilizer in vegetable gardens. Even today, suspended particles of rich soil from eroded banks of upland rivers are carried down the rivers, through the creeks of Winyah Bay and deposited in the salt marshes near North Inlet, which helps the growth of cordgrass.

Horry directed the use of the boats he owned—a small rowing boat, a larger sailing and rowing periagua and a flat for hauling heavy loads to and from his house in Georgetown to Dover Plantation and across Winyah Bay and Muddy Bay, through Jones Creek to North Island. Small boats of that time were either cypress dugout canoes or flat-bottomed wooden-planked bateaux, which could be rowed or sailed. Periaguas of that period were larger, up to fifty feet long, and either framed and planked or made from a cypress canoe with the bottom split and widened with planks and with the sides raised with planks. Periaguas usually had two masts and could be sailed or rowed. Flats were blunt-nosed, shallow-draft vessels, about forty or fifty feet long and twelve to fourteen feet wide with planked bottoms. Flats could carry heavy loads, even livestock, and were propelled by oars or by poling in shallow water.

Slaves built, loaded, operated and maintained Horry's boats. They were often seen being rowed or sailed with supplies, goods and even newspapers and mail back and forth from Georgetown or Dover Plantation, where his gardens furnished produce for North Island. Fruits were traded back and forth between island families as they became available from their plantations. Meat for his table was furnished by the island butcher, who brought as many as thirty head of cattle to the island at the beginning of the season and killed and butchered them as needed. Pigs were also brought over and ran wild across the island, scavenging for food, sometimes eating the eggs of sea turtles when they found their nests. Horry also had chickens and ducks to care for, as well as domestic dogs and cats. Fresh water was supplied from shallow wells and from cisterns that collected rainwater from the roofs of houses.

Others of Horry's slaves either hauled the bulky Peter Horry around the island in his mule-drawn carriage or hoisted him onto a sedan chair to walk the beaches. Slaves fished for him with nets or lines and also gathered oysters and clams for his meals. Fish and shellfish of all kinds were plentiful at North Inlet and offshore. House slaves did the cooking, washing, drawing his bath water from the cistern into the wooden tub that he had brought from Georgetown, cutting his hair, pouring his wine and all other jobs that he wanted done.

On July 17, Horry noted a problem with insects:

I woke Soon enough but determined to rise in future by dawn of day for Several Reasons. I daily Kill flies when Setting at my Table; this morning being Clouddy & wet I Killed more than Usual, by Such means my House has not Superabundance of these Troublesome Insects. No flees as yet, & not many Musketoes at my house but near the woods, Southward of me & the marsh Road Leading to the Inlet are Great many.

Horry knew the names of all of the species of fish that were common around North Island, but two fish that he once saw were new to him. He wrote:

Fine Weather, & Mullets runs finely. I Saw this morning at Sea but near the beach two amazing Fish Large & almost Round. Swimmed near the Surface of the water. I knew it not. Perhaps It may be a Devil fish. Such I have heard Off. Many Persons both Whites & black Came to behold Such Monstrious Large fishes & we all Stared at Such Uncommon fishes.

Devil fish, or manta rays, are still common near North Inlet.

Horry kept track of the weather, and on July 27, he noted the approach of a gale and gave advice to mariners:

Wind very high at North East for Sometime past & now tis heavy, Drisligg Cloudy weather. I look for a heavy Gale from the North East, or East Quarter & directly from Sea. So Marriners on our Coasts be Vigilent on board your Vessells Keep all Lights & Sails Close reefed & Bowlings all Clear, boats Secured on Deck & Experienced men, at your helm & Good Night watch, & Lights in Benecles to See your Compass & then I & you will Expect to Weather all.

August 1, 1812, was a special day for Peter Horry because he had been asked by the troop commander, Captain Gasqui, to review the 160 troops of the South Carolina State Militia who were stationed on North Island to protect Georgetown from possible invasion by the British and were living in tents at the south end of the island. Horry had a seven-mile journey to the south end of the island to review the troops. Traveling on the island by land was easiest at low tide, when he could ride on firm wet sand that would support the wheels of his carriage and the hooves of his mules. There was also an inland road of loose, dry sand along the length of the island, which often caused carriage wheels to bog down or to break the traces of his mules. His footman, Scipio, hurried his mules along the beach toward the south end of the island.

An hour later, they were within sight of the new brick lighthouse, a solid white cone that towered seventy-five feet above the beach. It had been completed earlier that year, replacing the wooden lighthouse that had been blown down by a hurricane in 1806.

Horry was impressed by the sturdiness and high quality of the masonry structure. Later that year, although the climb to the top was hard for a fat old man, Horry conducted a tour of ladies to the top to be amazed by the bright lamps in the lantern room. In his journal, he stated, "I with Mrs. Gasqua & Miss Henderson went to see the Lighthouse, the Pilot Conducted these Ladies to the Glasses or Lamps which Gives light at Night, no wood about the Light House all is brick or Stone & the Invention is admirable & well Executed." Horry always liked to be in the company of ladies—young ladies in particular. "I love young Women and girls, but I Cant Love old Women tho' I Venerate them." He was even tempted by sin: "She was Inviting, & I felt myself but alas, the Thought of Sinning (Altho' the Devil Tempted me) prevailed & my better Sense Predominated."

Several other families from North Inlet had come to picnic and watch the military maneuvers. Peter Horry was dressed in his general's uniform and was disappointed that many of the men lacked uniforms and paraded in homespun clothes. However, he was pleased that they tried their best to look military, and they made special gestures of esteem to Horry. After the parade and military maneuvers, Horry was invited by some of the officers to stay for dinner:

> *I drank more wine (say very Good) this day than I had Drunk for a year Past. I was really merry for my head ached at night, proved this Assertion. I Got home about 8 at Night & found my Bathing Tub Ready for me & my boat hauled up & Ready for Caulking & painting tomorrow. Keith gave us an Elegant Dinner & we drank I Suppose about 2 dozen of wine in 2 hours.*

Horry again visited the soldiers' camp near the lighthouse on August 16. There was a parade in the afternoon with many spectators, both men and women. Horry spotted Joseph Alston, the brigadier general in command of the state militia, whom he had not seen in several years. Alston had a summer home, called The Castle, at DeBordieu, just north of North Inlet. Horry made no effort to greet Alston, although he would have liked to have offered his condolences on the recent loss of Alston and Theodosia's young son. Horry guessed that Alston was too proud to advance toward him, and pride also prevented Horry from courting the favor of Alston, so they did not meet.

Alston's wife, Theodosia Burr Alston, was born in Albany, New York, in 1783, the daughter of prominent attorney Aaron Burr and Theodosia Prevost Burr, who died when her daughter was eleven years old. Young Theodosia spent most of her unmarried life in New York City with her charismatic, influential father, who saw to it that she was highly educated and would stay his closest confidante and mistress of his estate, Richmond Hill. When she was seventeen, she married Waccamaw rice planter Joseph Alston and moved to South Carolina, delaying for a day to watch Aaron Burr's inauguration as vice president. Their only son, Aaron Burr Alston, was born in 1802. Because of the difficult birth and other complications, Theodosia never completely recovered physically. Theodosia divided her time between her plantation on the Waccamaw, The Oaks, and visits with her father. In 1804, Aaron Burr fought a duel and killed Secretary of the Treasury Alexander Hamilton, whose insult to Burr may have been an

Theodosia Burr Alston by John Vanderlyn (1775–1852), oil on canvas, circa 1802, after a portrait in the Yale University Art Collection. *Courtesy of Brookgreen Gardens Archives.*

insinuation that he had an incestuous relationship with Theodosia. Following the duel, Burr's reputation was destroyed. He entered into a grandiose scheme to establish his own kingdom in the Southwest, to be assisted by Joseph and Theodosia. Burr's plans were discovered by President Thomas Jefferson, and he was denounced as a traitor and fled to Europe. Alston denied having anything to do with the plot and was exonerated. Burr finally returned to New York in 1812, a broken and poverty-stricken man.

After the death of her son from malaria in June 1812 at their beach house, The Castle, Theodosia left DeBordieu for the last time. Although not well, she was determined to visit her father in New York. Less than a month before she left, Joseph Alston was elected governor. Theodosia was first lady of South Carolina until December 1812, when she boarded the privateer schooner *Patriot* in Georgetown, headed for New York, but was lost in a storm at sea. She was only twenty-nine. Joseph Alston died in 1816 at the age of thirty-seven. The ruins of Joseph and Theodosia Alston's summer beach home are located on land now owned by Hobcaw Barony. In an overgrown clearing near the beach, a pile of handmade bricks from a fallen chimney is all that is left, but you can still feel the presence of the ghosts of Theodosia and her son.

During the summer of 1812, Horry visited and was visited by many of his friends and neighbors. On August 20, some of the soldiers from the encampment marched past his house on their way to review other troops at North Inlet. Horry loved to tell stories of his war experiences to anyone who would listen. During that summer, he attended a wedding on the island and heard several ministers preach sermons at various private homes. There was no church on the island as yet, but one would be built soon. Horry often conversed with fellow planters, some who had attended Harvard or Princeton, preparing to be lawyers, but had found it more profitable to become rice planters instead. Horry worried about his money and his rice crop and often corresponded by mail with his factor in Charleston.

Although Horry was not a man to over imbibe very often with wine or other spirits, he was often in the company of men and women who drank copiously, which was one of the diversions of summer life on North Island. On one occasion, Horry had a visit from a prominent Georgetown lawyer, Thomas R. Mitchell. Horry wrote:

Rode out & Got Some wood & returned home found Mr. Mitchell at my house. He Stayed & Breakfasted with me, however before he did so; he Asked for a Julep; my servant Rachael handed him, Brandy Sugar & water. I Soon founded 'fected his head, he Eat very Little at breakfast; a Decanter of Brandy, he Ordered to be placed on a Small Table Near to the One on which we were breakfasting on. He had frequently recourse to this decanter & Soon he realed to & fro. Laid down in a Room on a bed frequently, I found his Language, was Extremely defective, he Stammered, & his Eyes half Closed. At this Instant he is Asleep on a Bed in a Spare Room. I Gave Rachael directions not to Wake him, As he Spoke of Swimming in the sea.

A Shark would soon Cut him to pieces. I Sincerely Pity this Otherwise most Valuable Gentleman Planter & Attorney at Law but Alas he is Lost to himself, his friends & Country. Liquor, Oh Liquor what Mischief has thou Occasioned in the World.

In 1820, Thomas R. Mitchell, a Harvard graduate and great nephew of Francis Marion, defeated Benjamin Huger in an election for the U.S. Congress and served four terms between 1821 and 1833 as a staunch advocate of South Carolina's slave economy.

Most of the time, Horry treated his house slaves with kindness. They were given adequate food and clothing. On a few occasions, he allowed the children of house slaves to bathe in his tub. When a child of one of his wife's favorite slaves became sick at Dover Plantation, he allowed him to come to his North Island house, and he and his other slaves nursed him back to health. He depended on his house slaves for almost everything. On July 18, he wrote:

I was left with only Susie & Rachael (I cannot say too much of these two Servants, the former Acts towards me as a Mother & the Latter as a Sister, at All hours they attend to my Calls with Cheerfulness & tenderness used towards me. I wish I may ever have it in my Power to Reward their attention to me, few Negroes possess a Sense of Gratitude, these were born on my Plantation & brought up by my hands—I will ever Acknowlege their Goodness to me).

On August 30, he noted, "I am in the hands of Negroes & two of my house Wenches, Susie & Rachael are Kind to me. I may Say they are my Sisters & tends me as a Child (so helpless am I) they therefore are my Tryed friends, & they are found not wanting."

The year 1812 would be the last one that Peter Horry spent on North Island. In 1813, Horry moved into a house he had built in Columbia, and he died there in 1815, without heirs. What happened to his slaves after he died is not clear. His will of 1815 listed his slaves and placed a dollar value on each one. Although he spent most of his time in the company of his slaves, he seemed to have had no feelings regarding the morality of slavery, and he accepted the practice as a matter of course, just as did all of the other residents of North Island and the planters of Waccamaw Neck. He, like the others, treated slaves as livestock, owned to perform, without question, all tasks prescribed by their masters. Slaves were sometimes taught

Christianity in the back of white men's churches, where pastors emphasized faithful obedience by slaves to their masters in return for promised rewards in heaven. As an example, Reverend Edmund Botsford, a Baptist preacher in Georgetown, who also owned a house on North Island, was addressing slaves and declared:

> *Let your master, the people of the world, and your fellow-servants see that you endeavor to live a pious, godly life, agreeable to your profession, in all honesty and sobriety. When you have an opportunity, talk to your fellow servants about their souls' concerns, and pray daily for their conversion. Guard against self-conceit. Humility is a lovely virtue, and shines nowhere more than in a servant. Be careful to attend public worship when you have opportunity, and be regular and strict in secret and family prayer. Live in love with your wives, and keep to them only. Be careful of your children, that they do not tell lies, use bad words, or steal. Learn to make home the most agreeable place to you, and then you will not want to ramble from one plantation to another, and so will be kept from many temptations and hurtful snares. Be attentive to your master's business, and obey him in all things, pray daily for him and his family.*

School education for slaves was not allowed because their reading of books might encourage escape or insurrection. As early as 1800, the South Carolina legislature had enacted laws that restricted movements and meetings of slaves and made it more difficult to free slaves. Because of the slaves' overwhelming numbers compared to the number of white families in the Waccamaw Neck area, slaves were carefully controlled and punished severely for trying to escape. House slaves were less likely to try insurrection or escape because of better treatment by masters than field laborers received. However, house slaves were often more intelligent and more likely to be successful in attempts to escape or get around the demands of their masters. House slaves on North Island were generally glad to be away from the unhealthy atmosphere of the riverfront plantations and were willing to do almost anything that their masters or mistresses demanded. Besides, escape from North Island would have been very difficult.

THE HURRICANE OF 1822

For the remainder of the War of 1812, North Island experienced little action. A few enemy warships and privateers sailed past the island on the way north or south. American navy ships sometime patrolled the coast near the island. The economy of Georgetown had been hit hard by the Embargo of 1807, which prohibited the import and export of goods from and to Britain. By 1815, the war was over, and almost everything was back to normal. In 1816, prominent planter and member of Congress Benjamin Huger announced an appropriation of $1,500 for fixing buoys and markers on Georgetown Bank and in Winyah Bay. Additional monies were spent for range markers, all in attempts to improve navigation through Winyah Bay. Sometimes, as many as five or ten sloops from the rice plantations, loaded with barrels of rice, were anchored in Winyah Bay near the lighthouse, sails furled, awaiting a suitable wind and tide to make the ocean passage around Cape Romain to Charleston's rice mills and loading docks. Other sloops, brigs, barks and schooners, loaded with barrels of naval stores (turpentine, pitch and tar) and other cargo, frequently passed North Island Lighthouse on their way to markets. Small boats were often seen sailing back and forth between Georgetown and North Inlet via Winyah Bay, Jones Creek and Town Creek, supplying the needs of North Island's summer residents. Almost all transportation in those days was by water.

The summer colony of houses on North Island continued to grow. A church, a school and almost one hundred houses had been built on North Island by 1820, most of them congregated in Lafayette Village at North

Inlet. Many of the houses were owned by Waccamaw Neck rice planters. Some were owned by white merchants and professionals from Georgetown, who would sometimes close their offices or stores for the summer. The majority of the five or six hundred summer residents on the island were slaves. They served as coachman, valet, butler, cook, gardener, driver, lady's maid, laundress, oarsman, steersman, carpenter, stockman, fisherman and other invented titles. Any of those jobs on North Island was preferable to a slave than remaining on the plantation and being a field hand or having some other summer plantation job. The death rate from diseases like yellow fever, malaria, smallpox and typhus for black children and adults working and living on rice plantations in summer was terrible. Field hands suffered the worst conditions, working long hours barefoot in high heat and humidity in water above their ankles. Infant mortality on rice plantations averaged over 20 percent.

House slaves were the top level of plantation slave society. House slaves were selected by the planters because of their submissive behavior, their intelligence and ability to learn the necessary skills and, in many cases, because of the lightness of their skin, lightened over generations by unwanted and unmentioned sexual intercourse between female slaves and white overseers or members of a planter's family. Although the wives of planters objected to their husbands' indiscretions, they still preferred house slaves who looked more like themselves. With three hundred slaves living near one another on an island only nine miles long, there was an interactive slave community. Families of slaves were usually kept together, so there were children and grandparents in addition to the working house slaves. Certainly, some planter families were more demanding of their slaves' time than others, but slaves must have had some free time, particularly on Sundays and in the evenings. Surely, they would have discussed their dissatisfaction with living without freedom. House slaves were in the unique position to observe the social lives of planter families and to realize that slaves were as human as their masters. In general, though, they saw no way to improve their condition other than by discreet coercion of their masters. They knew that if they pushed their masters too far, they were liable to be sent back to the plantation to labor in the rice fields. They lived the best they could, fishing from their masters' boats, catching the cool sea breezes and dreaming of freedom.

Between 1804 and 1820, the residents of North Island had been spared the ravages of serious hurricanes. In those days, there were no warnings that a hurricane might be coming. On September 10, 1820, the *Gazette* reported:

The wind blew tempestuously all day fluctuating between points ENE and NE, but more generally blowing from NE. About sunset the scene became truly awful, the wind increasing in violence, and the tide running with frightful impetuosity. About this period, the church was blown from its foundations, and many of the inhabitants were seen removing from such houses as appeared most exposed to the dangerous tide and wind. After dark the gale continued to increase, and about 10 or 11 o'clock, there raged one of the most violent hurricanes that has been experienced here. At this hour the wind began to back (as it is called) to the N, blowing at times in squalls of incredible violence, bringing with them such floods of rain, that there was not a house in the village could entirely resist their fury. The wind about 1 o'clock appeared to have backed as far as NW from which quarter it continued to blow, but with decreasing violence until morning.

There were no deaths reported from the hurricane of 1820. Repairs were made to the damaged houses and the church during 1821.

When winter came, North Island was almost deserted. Each night, the lonely lighthouse keeper lit the lanterns at the top of the lighthouse. Moonlit nights cast shadows of the lighthouse across the sand. On cold winter nights and days, stormy nor'easter winds flattened the gray marsh grasses and rolled high tide waves against the dunes. On calmer days, the surf, the wind through trees and the cries of sea gulls were the only sounds that were heard. During the winter of 1821–22, only a few ships arrived in or departed from Georgetown and needed the North Island pilot, who kept his schooner tied up in a protected creek. The long winter finally turned to early spring, and sandpipers scurried along low tide beaches, pecking in the sand.

Lafayette Village came alive in April and May 1822. Birds nested, wildflowers bloomed, mullets jumped in the basin and marsh grasses turned to green. Slaves, some singing to their rhythms, rowed, poled and sailed boats and flats from plantations along the Waccamaw and from Georgetown across Winyah Bay and through Jones Creek to the North Inlet landings in front of the their owners' summer homes. Carpenters brought tools to make repairs and paint houses and piazzas. Laborers dug pits for new privies and cleaned stalls for the animals. Mules, horses, cattle, hogs, chickens and ducks were ferried over and put into their stables or pens. House slaves brought utensils, bedding, furnishings, candles, supplies, wine, brandy and food staples to the houses and cleaned and put things in their places. Finally, family members were rowed across the bay to their landings, along with their clothing, children's toys, games, books and personal items. There was much excitement as family members reclaimed their spaces, walked on the beach and began to relax for the summer. Family members greeted neighbors they hadn't seen since the previous summer. Cooks and servants were busy in the kitchen buildings, preparing their masters' first meals of the summer. Men sat on their verandas and were served juleps or sherry. A few smoked cigars and worried about their rice crops, hoping that their overseers would see to it that the field slaves' tasks were done properly. Most of these aristocratic ladies and gentlemen looked forward to a leisurely summer of socializing.

The men of Lafayette Village were united in their determination to continue the slave economy and to oppose all federal attempts to limit their rights. The planters favored an aristocratic republic, and they had the power to control the politics of the whole state. They violently opposed efforts by some members of Congress to increase federal controls and to legislate slavery out of northern territories. When planters on North Island got together that summer, they discussed with growing concern the problem of Negro uprisings and insurrection. They talked of the murder by Negroes of a Black River planter in May 1821. They thought it probable that their slaves had never learned about that incident. (It wouldn't be until 1823 that the four Negro culprits would be caught, hanged and their severed heads placed on poles as a warning to others.) The June 1822 Denmark Vesey uprising plot to murder whites and take over the city of Charleston was of much greater concern to the planters, even though twenty-three of the Negro plotters had been caught, convicted and hanged by the end of July. It was probable that the house slaves of North Island had learned about that incident. The planters and their families waited anxiously for current news from letters and newspapers brought from Georgetown by boat. The men worried about the safety of their women and children, as well as themselves, because of the Negroes' overwhelming numbers and their desire for freedom.

Life went on that summer much as it had in previous summers. Slaves were sent out into North Inlet basin in small boats to catch shrimp and mullets with net or seine, to catch crabs and stone crabs or to gather oysters and clams at low tide, all brought back to kitchens and prepared by the cooks for the owners' family dinners. Slaves fished for their masters with lines or nets for whiting, croakers, black fish and bass, using mullet or shrimp for bait. Turtle eggs were a delicacy if they were recovered before being eaten by a raccoon or hog. Some turtles were made into soup. Sometimes, a pilau was prepared using rice, okra and chicken, ham or shrimp. Salting or drying was the only way of preserving food. When catfish or sharks were caught, they were given to the slaves for their meals, along with rice, corn, vegetables and occasionally chicken, pork or beef. Boats from the plantations brought rice, potatoes, corn, tomatoes, squash, see wee beans, snap beans, okra, butter and salt to the island. When delicacies like honey, watermelons, tamarinds, Malaga grapes or figs were brought from a plantation, they were shared with neighbors. An apple dumpling, prepared by a neighbor's cook, made a fine desert.

Beef was usually bought from the island butcher, who brought calves and cattle to the island in the spring. Hogs that ran wild were killed when needed. Occasionally, deer, wild turkeys or quail were shot. Killing ducks was a winter sport, but domestic ducks and chickens were fed in their pens and killed for the table. Slaves fed and watered all of the animals, including horses, mules, dogs and cats. Water from shallow wells and from cisterns that caught rain from roofs was used to water animals and wash clothes and dishes. Water was brought in jugs from the mainland to be used for drinking straight or mixed with tea, coffee, brandy, rum or whiskey to make juleps and other drinks. Much wine, some imported and some made on the plantations, was consumed during the summer.

During that summer of 1822, many parties, dinners and dances were held at Lafayette Village. The weather had been fine for ten days in mid-September. On September 26, the Robert Withers family gave a housewarming party for their new house on the beach at Lafayette Village. The *Gazette* later reported:

> *Plenty of seafood was available as young women in gowns danced in candlelight to music from violins and drums. No one paid any attention to just another summer squall but as the rain came down in bucketful's and the tide rose quite high, they became alarmed and started abandoning the house for higher sand dunes. While many were still inside, the water lifted the new house off its foundations and slowly it drifted out to sea. All of its lights were burning in the darkness like a funeral pyre.*
>
> *At the time of high water…about seven o'clock in the evening, the inhabitants apprehended no danger from the tide, as, from the violence of the gale, it was presumed that it could not continue until the period of the succeeding high water. In this expectation, however, it pleased the Almighty to disappoint them, and by the awful result, to prove how fallacious are all human calculations.*
>
> *The tide could have ebbed little at all, when the waters returned with irresistible violence, and between 3 and 4 o'clock in the morning had reached a height far exceeding that of the gale of 1804, and we believe any other tide within the memory of the oldest inhabitants—a very small portion of North Island remained above the ocean. The gale began to subside we*

believe, about half after 3 o'clock, the wind blowing from the S.W. It was oppressively warm during the gale, and many of those luminous bodies, or meteors, unusual in our fall gales, passed near the surface of the earth. The gale was of shorter duration and accompanied by less rain than usual.

North Inlet itself and the floors of all the houses of Lafayette Village were well under water at the height of the storm. As men and women scrambled in the darkness toward safety, they might have seen a faint glow from the distant lighthouse, reflected from the bottoms of thick black clouds. On that night, whales at sea, whose brothers' flesh burned in the lighthouse lamps, had their day of reckoning. The planters and their families climbed to the roofs of their houses or swam and ran toward the safety of higher ground. There were high sand dunes on the island, but they were far away from Lafayette Village. Many of the slaves, who were trapped in their rooms under their masters' houses or in shacks behind the houses, had no place to go and were either drowned by the ocean surge or washed out to sea. Approximately 120 slaves on North Island were lost (31 are mentioned below). Some of them were children, and others were midwives who had nursed the children of planters. A few of the drowned slaves may have been blood relatives of the planters' own families. The house slaves who were lost were the most valuable assets of a rice planters' property. Sixteen white members of planter families at Lafayette Village (mentioned below) died in the storm. The total loss of life from the storm was about 300, including many slaves who were trapped in the low delta between the North and South Santee Rivers, a few miles south of Winyah Bay. Much of the livestock on the island also drowned.

The October 7, 1822 issue of the *City Gazette* described the damage to the Withers House (comments in brackets are gathered from Roy Talbert's and Meggan Farish's book about Peter Horry, George Rogers's book *The History of Georgetown County* and Alberta Lachecotte's book about Georgetown rice plantations):

R.F. Withers [Robert Francis Withers owned Silver Hill rice plantation on the Sampit River]—*The Dwelling House, a very large new building destroyed and not a vestige remaining—here again it is our melancholy duty to state the loss of many valuable lives—there were in this House Eighteen persons, of whom four have been most miraculously saved; those saved are Mr. R.F. Withers and three Negroes—those lost, we lament to say, are Mrs. Withers, her four amiable daughters, her son, Mr. Withers Shackelford, nephew of Mr. Withers, Mr. Wish, and five Negroes. Mr.*

Withers, about day-light, was heard calling for help in DeBourdieu's creek (near the ocean), a little above the settlement on that Island, and was rescued we understand by Lieut. Levy of the US Navy; it appears that he had clung to a piece of timber; Mr. Withers who had been long in a very bad state of health, finding himself chilled and exhausted called to one of his Negro men, who was endeavoring to gain the timber but whom he did not know, to secure himself on it, as he was about to relinquish it through inability to contend any longer; at this moment he heard the voice of his affectionate little son of twelve or thirteen years of age, of whose presence he was before ignorant, cheering him and entreating him to persevere in his exertions and assuring his father that he believed he, himself would be able to retain his grip of the timber till it should please God to cast them on shore—this instantly restored to the father animation and strength, but in a few minutes after an overwhelming surge separated them forever in this world. The Negro was afterwards taken up alive in the marsh opposite to that island; a Negro boy of Mr. Withers was driven across to DeBourdieu's Island on a pair of steps, landed and took refuge in a House which was shortly after blown down—he survives uninjured; another Negro man, whose arm was broken in the fall of the house has also been taken up alive.

Another account from the Johnstone Family History relates a story of Mrs. Andrew Johnstone (Sarah Elliott Mackewn), then living with her daughter Esther and son-in-law, Robert Francis Withers:

About 1815, she had a vivid dream one night while at their beach house on North Island. She saw in her dream that in a terrible storm her daughter and grand children had perished in the waves. She told the story the next morning and begged her son-in-law to sell and move far inland. After much persuasion, he followed her advice and moved inland to Statesburg, SC for the summers. In 1817 Mrs. Johnstone died and since the family had missed the sea so much they desired sometime later to purchase a lot and build on the water's edge. In 1822 it was their house warming party and their house that drifted out to sea with all candles burning, thus giving Esther and children a watery grave as had been foreseen seven years before by her mother.

The *City Gazette* continued:

A detailed account of the sufferings of families, or individuals, will not be attempted, for were it necessary, the state of our feelings, produced by the horrors of this dreadful night, and the scene of ruin and devastation which now surrounds us, would incapacitate us for the task. We hasten to give a brief account of the injuries sustained in the different dwellings:

Dr. Ford [his family owned the plantations Rice Hope, Waterford, Peru and Inland]—*His out buildings injured and piazza settled.* Dr. Allston [a physician who graduated from the University of Pennsylvania, a rice planter and owner of Arundel Plantation on the Pee Dee River who helped to plan and erect Prince Frederick Episcopal Church]—*kitchen blown down and servants' hall injured. S.W. Heriot*— *Servants' hall down and kitchen unroofed; stable partly so.* Rev. G. Capers [one of Georgetown's published authors; he wrote "A Discourse" in 1822]—*Kitchen and stables unroofed, much of the underpinning of the dwelling house washed down by the sea.* Robt. Heriot [graduated from Princeton University and was a merchant and planter near Georgetown; the Heriot family owned substantial portions of what became Hobcaw Plantation and several other plantations along the Waccamaw River]—*Dwelling house unroofed, doors and windows burst in, all piazzas and the shed-rooms blown away, the chimney fractured near the base and the top blown off, the family (with a child very ill) after the house was unroofed, fortunately obtained shelter in a neighboring dwelling; the family escaped though devine mercy without any other injury other than a contusion on the eye of an infant son.* B.F. Trapier [attended Harvard University and served as a captain during the American Revolution; he was the grandson of a founder of Georgetown and first owner of North Island]—*Servants' lodging blown down and stables partly unroofed.* Rev. M.H. Lance [rector of Prince George Winyah. During his lifetime, he owned Greenfield and Wedgefield rice plantations]—*Kitchen down and the chimney of the dwelling house.* Mrs. E. Myers [Levi and Moses Myers owned Exchange rice plantation]—*House nearly down and injured in the roof and gable end. Mrs. Sarxadas—Every building destroyed; the family took refuge in the house of Moses Fort, Esq., where three of them afterwards lost their lives, a white child and two servants. R.A. Taylor—every building down. T.F. Goddard—Piazzas and sheds destroyed, out buildings damaged. L. Salomon—House and kitchen chimneys down.* A. Marvin [a director of the Georgetown branch of the Bank of South Carolina, member of the Georgetown Library Society and agent for the American Seaman's Friend Society]—*Out buildings destroyed. P.*

Cuttino [a director of the Georgetown branch of the Bank of South Carolina and a Baptist preacher to blacks and whites in Georgetown]—*House chimney down; piazza roof partly off, out buildings injured. Mrs. Henry—Every building demolished. Rev. J.S. Capers—Piazza injured. I. Solomons—Piazza injured. Lizar Joseph* [born in Mannheim, Germany; a Jewish businessman who owned a wharf in Georgetown and was secretary of the Winyah Indigo Society]—*Part of piazza and stable injured. Gen. T. Carr* [owned a rice plantation on the Pee Dee River and was intendant (mayor) of Georgetown in 1813 and 1814]—*Dwelling house chimney down, and kitchen piazza blown away. Mrs. Savage Smith* [Savage Smith was intendant of Georgetown in 1808 and a successful planter with two hundred slaves; he was president of the state senate and was commissioner to superintend the cutting of a canal across North Island in 1805, along with other commissions to provide state-financed internal improvements]—*Stables and fish house destroyed. L.L. Josephs—Dwelling house down and torn to pieces, out buildings injured. Mrs. Thurston—House down, out buildings damaged. Thomas Herlot—Buildings destroyed and carried off by the water. The church destroyed and every vestige carried off by the water. H. Inglesby—Kitchen piazza blown away. Mrs. Blyth* [probably the aunt of R.F.W. Allston, whose family owned the plantation Waties Point]—*kitchen piazza blown away. J.M. Taylor* [a graduate of Harvard and owner of Mansfield Plantation on the Black River; he was an incorporator of the Pee Dee Steamboat Company and a director of the Georgetown branch of the Bank of the State of South Carolina]—*Dwelling house down. Dr. Thomas—Carriage house and stables down. J.C. Coggeshall—Dwelling house settled at one end. John Porter, Jr.* [intendant of Georgetown in 1823]—*Dwelling house much wrecked and out buildings injured. A. DeRoss—Building destroyed and carried away by the water; this benevolent, industrious and honest man, and a Negro lad, the only inhabitants, are both lost. Moses Fort—Every outbuilding destroyed, the Dwelling House thrown from its foundation, shattered and removed some distance; the piazzas and sheds blown away. In this house there were five deaths, to wit: Mrs. Hannah Botsford, the relict of the late Rev. Edmund Botsford* [a leading Baptist in the Georgetown community who wrote "Sambo and Toney," which was designed to teach Christian lessons to the slaves]—*Miss Scott, the daughter of David Scott, and three servants were lost.*

Dr. L. Myers [the Myers and Salomon families were prominent Jewish families who were important in the economic life of Georgetown in the early 1800s; Dr. Levi Myers earned a medical degree from the University of Glascow and was the first Jewish doctor to hold a membership in the Medical Society of South Carolina]—*Every building torn to pieces by the sea and every vestige of them destroyed, and this respectable and worthy man with every member of his amiable family drowned. In this house, fifteen lives were lost, to wit: Dr. Myers, Mrs. Myers, three Daughters and a Son, and nine servants.*

The few boats that have been recovered are used in searching for the bodies of the deceased and removing them to town. Before we close this brief statement, we will merely state that the buildings at the south end of the North Island are much injured, but that no lives have been lost. At Debourdieu's Island the havoc has been less, but many Negroes have been drowned and crushed by the falling of buildings. We understand that Wm. A. Alston, Esq. [called "King Billy," he was one of the biggest slaveholders in All Saints Parish; he owned various plantations on the Waccamaw River, including Fairfield, Clifton, Weehawka, Claremont, Midway, Crabhall, Strawberry Hill, Rose Hill and Bellfield; George Washington visited Alston in 1791]—*has lost on this island eleven Negroes.*

There were a few planter families living on Pawleys Island, a few miles north of North Inlet, during the summer of 1822, but no deaths were reported there. One of the Pawley family's first American ancestors, Percivell Pawley, was mentioned in an early family Bible: "Thursday the 14th of November 1723 my father Percivell Pawley drowned at ye North Inlate about 9 or 10 a Clock at nite—being 50 years old & was very harty & healthy."

Despite the huge amount of damage to all buildings on North Island, with the exception of the solid masonry Georgetown Lighthouse, which was used as a sanctuary by those nearby, many of the planters had their houses rebuilt. In 1823, a number of storm-proof circular brick towers were built on North Island, South Island and at the mouth of the Santee to afford protection for slaves in the future. Some of these structures were still standing in 1893, when another hurricane disaster struck, and two of them still stand today.

Summer life on the island continued much as before the hurricane of 1822, until the beginning of the Civil War. In 1825, R.S. Green advertised his school at North Inlet in a Georgetown newspaper. In 1826, the eighteen-year-old daughter of the owner of Keithfield Plantation died on North Island. Robert Mills wrote in 1826, "To accommodate the population which collect, during each summer, on North Island, a church has been erected there. The number of persons which assemble on this island, at this season, is between 600 and 700." In 1832, Paul Trapier died on North Island. In 1832, Lockwood described North Island in his geography book as "equally delightful as to aspect, society and healthfulness."

In 1834, another hurricane struck North Island. "The tide, impelled by a tornado, rose to unparalleled heights and destroyed seven dwelling houses and one church and 37 lives were lost." In 1838, the Ladies of North Island gave a "Pic Nic" celebration of the Fourth of July, with orations and culinary arts, which included ice cream. In 1841, Mr. John Porter, eldest son of Colonel John Porter, died at his North Island home in the twentieth year of age. William Chapman died on North Island that same year.

In 1851, an advertisement for the sale of a shipwreck that occurred on North Island appeared in the *Winyah Observer*:

> *Uderwriters Sale, Schooner* PHENIX *& Cargo of Lumber by Thomas R. Sessions & Co. To-morrow, the 4th inst at 10 o'clock A.M. will be sold on North Island Beach for a'c underwriters and all concerned. The Schr* PHENIX *as she now lies with her SAILS, RIGGING, ANCHORS, CHAINS & CARGO OF LUMBER. Conditions—Cash*

NORTH ISLAND LIGHTHOUSE

The United States Congress had appropriated funds in 1810 to build a solid masonry lighthouse at North Island on the site of the wooden one, which blew down in 1806. Starting in 1811, a contractor from Charleston had been busy with crews of black slaves, hauling and laying half a million bricks "of the best South Carolina kind." The walls of the lighthouse were five and a half feet thick for the lower sixteen feet of height, four and a half feet thick for the next fourteen feet, three and a half feet thick for the next twelve feet, three feet thick for the next eleven feet, two and a half feet thick for the next ten feet and two feet thick for the top nine feet. The outside walls of the lighthouse were plastered with mortar and painted white. A spiral stair to the top of the lighthouse had four landings and was built from 120 carved stone steps, which extended six inches into the wall and formed a pillar in the center of the lighthouse. Small windows were placed on opposite walls at each revolution of the stairs. The lantern was made of cast-iron plates and was eight feet in diameter and nine feet high from the floor to the roof. The exterior edge of the lantern gallery was surrounded by a wrought-iron railing. The grade-level floor was constructed of brick pavers in a herringbone pattern. The lighthouse keeper lived in a house next to the lighthouse. Barrels of whale oil were stored in a nearby fireproof outbuilding. Each evening, the lighthouse keeper's slave hauled whale oil up the stone steps of the lighthouse to the iron lantern room at the top, and the keeper lit the lamps. Ships approaching Winyah Bay from the north or south could see the light from North Island Lighthouse from ten miles out to sea.

North Island Lighthouse. *Photograph by Phil Wilkinson.*

During the 1820s, Captain Moses Rogers, who had commanded the *Savannah*, the first steamship to cross the Atlantic, established the first South Carolina steamboat line in Cheraw that hauled freight and passengers up and down the Pee Dee River and other rivers to Georgetown without regard to current or wind. During the 1830s, 1840s and 1850s, numerous steamboats carried rice, lumber, naval stores and cotton from upriver plantations to Georgetown and returned with supplies for the plantations. Steamboats began to make outside passages from Georgetown to Charleston. Steam tugboats towed loaded sailing ships in and out of Winyah Bay, past North Island Lighthouse and into the Atlantic Ocean, where they spread their sails and made passages to northern ports or to the West Indies or Europe. Rice, the most profitable commodity, was still shipped directly from the Waccamaw Neck rice plantations to Charleston, where it was processed and shipped to market. From 1840 to 1860, between 25 to 50 percent of all rice grown in America was grown in the Georgetown District. The lighthouse guided hundreds of vessels toward the entrance to Winyah Bay.

The lighthouse, completed in 1812, was subject to periodic inspection by Mr. Winslow Lewis. In 1837, Winslow Lewis, the inventor of the Lewis lighthouse lamp, was a lighthouse construction contractor who had an exclusive contract with Stephen Pleasonton, overseer of the U.S. Treasury Department's Lighthouse Establishment, to maintain and furnish lamps

A steam tugboat towing a bark out of Winyah Bay. *Courtesy of Michael and Ginny Prevost.*

for all lighthouses along the entire East Coast. Congress had appointed Pleasonton to his position as a reward for physically saving an original copy of the Declaration of Independence from destruction by fire when the British burned down the Capitol during the War of 1812. Lewis wrote a letter to Pleasonton, describing all that he said was wrong with the North Island Lighthouse and the keeper's house, and offered to make all repairs for $6,000. Pleasonton wrote back:

> *The repairs which you state to be necessary are much more extensive than I had any idea of. The plan securing the foundation I think an excellent one, and will durably protect the Lighthouse. In addition to this it appears that an entirely new lantern and soapstone deck are wanted, as well as new lamps and reflectors; a new dwelling house; the kitchen requires raising and repairing; and the tower of the light house needs rough casting with roman cement and whitewashing, etc.*

The repairs to North Island Lighthouse were made in 1838. In 1844, it was reported that the North Island lighthouse had eleven Lewis lamps with nine-inch reflectors. Lewis continued his exclusive "sweet deal" contract with Pleasonton until 1850, when Lewis died. A much more efficient lens for lighthouse lamps had been invented and developed by Augustin Fresnel in France in 1820, but Pleasonton considered them "too expensive" and stuck with Lewis lamps and reflectors

A photograph of the Fresnel lens that lit the North Island Lighthouse from 1868 until 1986. *Courtesy of the South Carolina Maritime Museum and Grand Strand Pilot.*

until 1850. After that time, all lighthouses replaced their Lewis lamps with Fresnel lenses.

In 1855, an efficient fourth-order Fresnel lens, manufactured in Paris, was installed in the lantern room of North Island Lighthouse, eighty feet above the base. Fresnel lenses were classified in size by order, a first-order lens being the largest and ranging down to the smallest, an eleventh-order lens. The source of light, the lantern, was located inside the Fresnel lens. The glass prisms of the lens concentrated and projected white light from the lantern, 360 degrees around and twelve miles out to sea. The lantern, fueled with oil, was lit each day at dusk. An 1855 statement of finances said, "Georgetown, Ocracoke, Sapelo and St. Augustine reported saving on oil, wicks and other items, where lenses have been substituted for reflectors, the percentage of oil, wicks, and chimneys saved has, I am satisfied, been more than 80/100."

There were no lighthouses between Winyah Bay and Morris Island, in Charleston, until 1827, when a lighthouse was built on Raccoon Cay, near Cape Romain, to warn ships of the dangerous shoals off Cape Romain, six miles away from the lighthouse. Winslow Lewis built the first Cape Romain Lighthouse, which was similar in construction to the North Island Lighthouse

The Cape Romain Lighthouses and keeper's house. *Courtesy of the Georgetown County Digital Library.*

but shined a red light out to sea. It was not tall enough to be effective, so in 1857, an impressive 150-foot brick lighthouse was built near the other one. The second Cape Romain lighthouse carried a first-order Fresnel lens in its lantern room, the white beam of which could be seen eighteen miles out to sea. The lens for that lighthouse was destroyed by Confederates during the Civil War but was repaired in 1866. Subsequently, the lighthouse tower began to settle and lean to one side, developed cracks and was discontinued in 1947. The abandoned tower can still be seen from several miles offshore during daylight hours. One problem with that lighthouse was that ships a few miles off the coast and traveling from north to south, after passing North Island Lighthouse, sometimes mistook the Cape Romain Lighthouse for the lighthouse in Charleston and turned toward the shoals of Cape Romain before realizing their mistake. Offshore markers on the shoals of Cape Romain replaced the lighthouse, but these shoals still claimed several ships and remain the most dangerous obstruction between Charleston and the coast of North Carolina.

CIVIL WAR AND THE END OF SLAVERY

Throughout the 1840s and 1850s, the wealthy rice planters of Waccamaw Neck, including the Allston, Alston and Ward families, met each summer on North Island with increasing anxiety to discuss the approaching crisis, which was being brought to a head by abolitionists and others who wanted to interfere with their state's right to determine their own future. By 1860, there were eighteen thousand slaves and only two thousand whites in the Georgetown District. The planters were completely dependent on a slave economy to support their lifestyle. Believing that Abraham Lincoln's election would lead to the end of their slave economy, the rice planters of Waccamaw Neck were instrumental in bringing about South Carolina's secession from the Union, to become part of a new slave-owning nation. When Lincoln refused to allow the secession of Southern states, war was inevitable. The first shots of the Civil War were fired across Charleston Harbor in April 1861. Starting that summer, the rice planters of Waccamaw Neck had few opportunities to take vacations on North Island.

Preparations for the defense of Georgetown Harbor had been started in January 1861. Lieutenant LeBleux was assigned the responsibility of preparing defenses on the south end of North Island. Cannon emplacements, a redoubt and a powder magazine were completed, and similar defenses were built on South Island and Cat Island to protect the entrance to Winyah Bay. Several planters joined the military as officers to lead white citizen volunteers, who enlisted for short terms, confident that they would be able to defend their land and quickly defeat the Yankees. On January 23, Colonel Alston wrote to the Confederate secretary of war, "The work at North Island to be immediately occupied by a detachment of Volunteer Artillery, and the island itself (being nine miles long) to be occupied by a few riflemen to communicate with a Patrol of Cavalry, stationed on the shore of the opposite island (South Island)." In February 1861, a detachment of the Third Regiment of South Carolina Artillery manned the defenses at North Island. In addition, it was suggested that a guard be placed in the lighthouse as a lookout for hostile vessels. The defenders of Winyah Bay expected an attack soon after the war began in April 1861, but instead, the Union forces bypassed Georgetown and Charleston and landed farther south at Port Royal, Hilton Head and Beaufort.

A serious blockade of Winyah Bay by the Union navy began in December 1861. The Union side-wheel steamer *James Adger* and the bark *Gem of the Sea* patrolled the South Carolina coast above Charleston. In December, the *Gem of the Sea* chased the British blockade-runner *Prince of Wales* into North Inlet after hulling it several times. The *Prince of Wales*'s captain set fire to the ship to keep it from falling into Union hands. A Confederate soldier stationed on North Island wrote to his wife about the incident:

> *Well the Yankees sent fire boats up the Inlet to the Burning Schooner to put out the fire and tow her off. Well it so happened that Lieu. Hailler of Company D who are stationed on North Island with six of his men were up the Beach Scouting and concealed themselves behind the Sand Hills from where they fired upon them and drove them off. They had fixed a Rope to the schooner and were about to succeed in getting her off, but when Hailler fired on them they were in such a hurry to leave that they cut the Rope, they fired back at him but done no damage, they made a second attempt to land and he drove them off a second time. Well about 8 o'clock that night the Col wrote to Norman (the soldier's commanding officer) saying that he had received intelligence from a Messenger that the enemy had occupied North Inlet. Ordered us to double our Guard and be ready at a moment's notice for any emergency, the man who brought the letter said that there was one thousand or fifteen hundred of them. You may guess we had an exciting time.*

The company guarding North Island during the winter of 1861–62 was hard hit by sickness. Thirty-one soldiers who were stationed on North Island died in hospital of mumps, typhoid fever and dysentery. Colonel Alston continued to tell the men that there wasn't enough money to buy blankets for them, but the soldiers knew that Alston had chartered the Confederate side-wheel steamer *Nina* for $150 a day to carry him from Bulls Bay to Georgetown. During one winter storm, a Union supply steamer, carrying live cattle and other provisions toward their base at Beaufort, was wrecked on the Georgetown bar. Another steamer was disabled and captured by the *Nina*.

In April 1862, after a year of guarding the Winyah Bay entrance against attacks that never came, the soldiers there were ordered to abandon their positions and transfer to Robert E. Lee's command in the western theater. The guns on North Island and South Island were dismounted at night, and logs, called Quakers, were put in their place. Before the North Island defenses and the lighthouse were abandoned, the Confederates destroyed the lantern room of the lighthouse, prohibiting its use by the enemy. Soon afterward, Union forces occupied all of North Island.

In April 1862, the blockade runner *Liverpool* was forced onto the shore of North Inlet by the Union side-wheel steamer *Keystone State*. In May 1863, Union navy commander George Prentiss of the *Albatross* occupied the lighthouse, and the commander of another Union ship offshore reported, "On the following morning at 8 AM, we saw a flagstaff erected on the lighthouse, with the glorious flag of our Union attached to it." Union forces utilized the existing defenses on North Island and, in 1864, added a fort with a 30-foot-tall tower to use as a temporary lighthouse. Several blockade runners, especially during the first year of the war, succeeded in avoiding the blockading ships and brought their cargo into Georgetown. There, they loaded their ships with cotton, naval stores or rice and waited for a chance to escape back to sea. In March 1862, the largest blockade runner to avoid the blockading fleet and run past North Island into Georgetown on extreme high tide was the steamer CSS *Nashville*, 215 feet long and drawing 21 feet of water. It had been a U.S. Mail Service ship that was fired on and captured in Charleston at the beginning of the war. It was the first ship of war to fly the Confederate flag in England. It was sold and renamed the SS *Thomas L. Wragg*, renamed again the SS *Rattlesnake* and sunk in the Ogeechee River in 1863 by the Union ironclad USS *Montauk*.

After the defenses on North and South Islands were abandoned, Georgetown was largely undefended, and Union ships began to sail up Winyah Bay to Georgetown. In May 1862, two Union ships sailed past Georgetown and ten miles up the Waccamaw River to rice plantations, where they took eighty slaves, whom they called contrabands, on board and brought them back to North Island. Beginning in 1862, hundreds of contrabands were quartered on North Island as they were taken by the

Union forces or escaped from plantations and turned themselves over to the Union. Life on North Island was not easy for contraband families, which must have included women and children. There were few existing structures at the south end of the island for shelter and no sources of food other than what the Union soldiers could provide. It is probable that contrabands, as well as their Union soldier protectors, used some of the existing summer homes of the planters at North Inlet for shelter. The Union navy sent armed boats up the Waccamaw River to raid plantations for rice to feed the contrabands on North Island. Union soldiers probably treated contrabands little better than planter overseers had treated them as slaves. Also, there was fear that Confederate soldiers might try to attack the contrabands. The escaped slaves could only hope that their time as contrabands on North Island was a first step toward freedom. Contrabands were later transferred to the Union base at Port Royal, where they joined the Union army or were put to work in Union camps. Robert Blake, a Santee slave contraband who was brought to North Island, immediately enlisted in the Union navy and served as a steward on the Federal gunboat *Marblehead*. He distinguished himself in battle and was the first African American to receive the Medal of Honor. In June 1863, four hundred more contrabands were brought to North Island. Some of the Waccamaw Neck rice planters took their slaves farther inland to prevent them from being captured or from turning themselves over to the enemy.

In February 1865, after the fall of Charleston, the Union gunboats *Pawnee*, *Mingoe* and *Nipsic* crossed the bar into Winyah Bay, steamed up the bay, took over the abandoned fort at Battery White and steamed into Georgetown to accept surrender of the town. A few days later, the Union flagship *Harvest Moon*, commanded by Admiral John Dahlgren, anchored off Battery White. On March 1, after inspecting the abandoned fort, Admiral Dahlgren got underway in the *Harvest Moon*, struck a floating Confederate mine and sank in shallow water in Winyah Bay, with the loss of only one man. The sinking of the *Harvest Moon* was the only loss of a Union flagship during the Civil War. One month later, the war was over.

The 1811 lighthouse on North Island had been heavily damaged during the war. At the end of the war, before the United States Lighthouse Service could arrange to have it repaired, the Union fort and tower were used as a temporary lighthouse. An incident occurred there in 1866 that was described in a later *New York Sun* newspaper article:

> *During the last year of the war the lighthouse on North Island, at the entrance of Winyah Bay, on the coast of South Carolina, was destroyed*

by fire. The one erected to replace it temporarily was built by a party of Federal soldiers. It's height was about twenty-five feet, and the material used was stone, brick and timber. There wasn't much architecture about it, but it was solid enough for a fort. Indeed, it was built as a combination, and for several weeks was in charge of a sergeant of infantry and seven or eight men. Orders were finally received to leave two men in charge until relieved by an appointee of the Lighthouse Board. The name of my companion was George Wilson. We had an abundance of rations, two extra muskets, and plenty of ammunition, and aside from keeping the old-fashioned light in order, we had nothing to do. War was over, but the country was unsettled, and gangs of bad men were prowling along the coast as well as through the interior.

On the afternoon of the fourth day after the sergeant's departure a sloop which had probably come out of the Santee River approached us from the south and came to anchor just inside the island. She had six men aboard, and after fishing for an hour or so two of the crew came ashore in a small boat. Wilson was asleep at this time, and I had been watching them from the lantern room with the glass. I needed only one glance to prove that the crew of the sloop was a bad lot. The glass brought them so near that I could study each individual face and from the very first I made up my mind that the fishing was all a pretence. While they fished they furtively inspected the lighthouse, and as soon as the boat put out I roused up Wilson, and we went outside to receive the strangers. During the war many blockade runners had succeeded in getting into the port of Georgetown, at the head of the bay, but at least half a dozen had been driven ashore in our vicinity. There were then two wrecks on the east side of the island and two on the mainland, and unknown to us, a story was afloat that a large amount of English gold had been taken from one of the wrecks and deposited in the lighthouse for safe keeping until its rightful ownership could be decided. It was a very silly story, but found many believers. We had no means of getting at any of the wrecks, and had any considerable sum of money been found it would have been turned over to the Government, of course. I had time before the boat landed to tell Wilson what I thought about the men, and we agreed on what we should say and how we should act. Only one man came up to the lighthouse. Had he been encountered on the mainland he would have been called a guerrilla. He was a middle-aged man, with a fierce and crafty look, and his efforts to appear pleasant and pass off for a fisherman were lamentable failures. When we had saluted each other he said that he and his men were to wait where they were for a British bark called the Harvest

Home *to come out of Georgetown, when five of them were going to ship in her. He asked if we had any objections against their camping ashore for the night, and he wanted to buy bacon and coffee.*

I pretended that I would have to ask the sergeant before answering and turned and entered the lighthouse and closed and fastened the door behind me. We had met the stranger about forty feet from the door, and had planned not to let him enter the building and discover we were two alone. The fact must have already been known to them, however, or at least strongly suspected, for I had scarcely closed the door when the man knocked Wilson head over heels by a blow on the nose and dashed at the door. Let me tell you about the build of the lighthouse and you will get a clearer idea of my situation. The door was narrow and studded with boltheads. There was a loophole on either side for musketry. The ground floor room was circular, with walls over two feet thick. Ascent to the lantern room was made by means of wooden ladders. There was a circular walk around the lantern with a brick parapet four feet high. The lighthouse stood back 100 feet from high tide, and about the same distance in the rear of it was a ridge of sand and gravel running clear across the island. Here and there grew a bush and a patch of grass, but there were no trees within gunshot. The door opened inward and was secured by a heavy bar across the centre. I had intended to remain inside two or three minutes and then return and deliver a message from the sergeant, but when I heard someone kicking on the door I realized that the stranger had already shown his hand. From one of the loopholes I saw Wilson sprawled on his back and also noticed the small boat making off the sloop. Just then the stranger called through the other loophole:

"Look here, young fellow, don't you lose any time opening this door if you want to live to see sundown!"

"What do you want in here?" I asked.

"None of your business! You open the door or I'll show you no mercy!"

"You can't come in here!"

"Open this door, I say!" he shouted as he pounded on it with a stone.

The small boat was now coming ashore with the rest of the fellows, and Wilson was sitting up and looking around him in a dazed way. He did not get up until the men reached him. The leader of the gang left the door as they came up, and all gathered around Wilson for a consultation. After a few minutes he was tied hand and foot and deposited in the boat on the beach. Then the gang approached the door in a body, and the leader called to me:

"Come now, open this door! We know you are all alone in there, but we don't want bloodshed if it can be avoided. We have come after the money and are bound to have it."

"There's no money here. Ask my comrade and he'll tell you the same."

"But open the door and let us see."

"I shan't do it!"

The lighthouse was a place worth looting. We had three or four barrels of oil, a barrel of molasses, one of rice, half a barrel of sugar, two barrels of flour, a lot of bacon and hardtack, a barrel of coffee and other stuff. If the gang plundered the place they were not likely to leave two witnesses behind when they sailed away, nor was it probable that they would land us at any point where we could give an immediate alarm. The chances were at least even up that they would murder us to conceal their identity. Having served as a soldier for over three years and known the strength of the position I occupied, I was not at all frightened by the presence of the gang. A demand was again made on to me to open the door, and when I refused I knew pretty well what their first move would be. On the beach near their boat lay a piece of timber which the tide had stranded. They went for it at once, and in the hands of six stout fellows it would have proved a powerful battering ram. They had evidently made up their minds that I wouldn't dare shoot, for they came straight at the door with timber. Even when I thrust my musket through the loophole they paid no attention, but as I saw they were bound to batter the door in, I put a bullet into the right shoulder of the leader. He wasn't over fifteen feet away, and the bullet whirled him twice 'round and then pitched him headlong. Two of the gang seized him and pulled him aside, and then all got out of range. Every man of them had a knife and a pair of revolvers, but they soon discovered that numbers and weapons didn't count. There was no chance to fire on me except through the loopholes, and I was carefully watching one of those. They crept up to the other and fired five or six shots, but it was powder and ball thrown away.

It was about half past 5 o'clock in the afternoon when I was driven inside. Half an hour after the wounding of their leader they were ready to give it up as a bad job and return to their sloop. Their small boat lay directly in front of the door, and as they began moving toward it I fired and slightly wounded one of the men assisting the leader to get down to the beach. All of them at once hurried to the left to get out of range. It had struck me that if they had taken Wilson away they would murder him, and I determined to keep them from the boat. In a few minutes one of the gang came creeping around as near my loophole as he dared to demand my surrender. If I refused they would burn me out.

There being no drift stuff within a mile of us, I did not worry over his threat. As he retreated to the rear of the house to join his companions I saw

Wilson's head rise above the gunwale of the boat. Seeing the coast clear, he rose up, leaped out of the boat, and shoved her into the water. The tide was going out, and with the help of the oars he was soon aboard the sloop. I made my way to the lantern room to watch his movements and when I saw him handling a double barreled shotgun which he had brought from the cabin, I gave him a cheer which put the rascals below on the alert, and resulted in their discovery of what had occurred. The situation now presented was a curious one. I was a prisoner inside the lighthouse but the gang were prisoners outside as well. Wilson had captured both boat and sloop, and while he could render me no assistance he stood between the men and escape.

I expected to be fired on when I lighted the lantern, which was in an exposed position, and sure enough they did open on me with their revolvers and shaved me pretty close three or four times. I got down safely, however, and then had only the door to guard during the night. The fellows could not tell whether I had been hit or not, and about 9 o'clock I heard one of them at the loophole where I was watching and listening. I had a cocked revolver close at hand, and the yell which followed the report told me that he had been hit. What the four unwounded men would do during the night I could only guess at and be on the watch to checkmate. By 10 o'clock it was so dark I could not see the beach, and then two of them, as subsequently appeared, went down to the shore and undressed and swam off to capture the sloop. It was a daring thing to do, for the craft was a quarter of a mile away, the tide running strong, and the waters infested by sharks. Wilson not only found the shotgun, but a loaded revolver and a cavalry carbine, and he rightly reasoned that as soon as night came the gang would attempt to retake the sloop. Being at anchor and swinging with the tide, he knew that she could only be boarded at the bows, and he took his station there and was on the alert when the swimmers came off. One of them was swept past him and out to sea shouting for aid, and the other was shot as soon as he seized the forechains. I saw the flash and heard the shot, and Wilson afterward waved a lighted lantern as a signal to me that he was all right.

I, of course, could not tell how many of the gang had gone off to the sloop, and continued watchful for any move against the door. The two wounded men must have suffered a great deal, but the leader was a determined fellow and bound to get revenge if nothing more. He sent the two unwounded men back to the woods for fagots, and about midnight I heard sounds which made me suspicious. Of a sudden both loopholes were closed up by limbs being thrust into them, and the fagots were heaped against the door. I had anticipated this move and planned what to do. Before the fellows could fire the fagots, I opened on them from the parapet with my revolver, wounding both. It was not until two hours later, however, that I knew I had hit either one of them. I had managed to clear one of the loopholes when one of the gang crawled as near as he dared and shouted:

"Say yo' in thar! We want to surrender!"

"How many are there of you?"

"Four, and we are all wounded and suffering. The Captain will be a dead man unless he kin git help pretty soon?"

"Where are the other two?"

"They went off to the sloop and got shot. Say, mister, for heaven's sakes don't go back on us! We come to rob the place as I won't deny, but we've got the wust of it and want to cry quits."

I believed it was a plot to get me off my guard and refused to open the door. Twice more before daylight the same man came and appealed to me, but he received the same answer. When day broke I looked down on them from the parapet and saw that the leader was dead and the other three wounded. Before opening the door I made them discard their revolver and knives, and as I went out to them Wilson was coming ashore in the small boat. The Captain, as they called him, had bled to death, one of the men was wounded in the foot, another in the back, and the third in the knee, and they were as humble as you please. We bound up their wounds and made them as comfortable as possible, and that afternoon a Government steamer took them up to Georgetown. We had a good overhaul of the sloop before we let her go, and we made several surprising discoveries. She had about $500,000 of Confederate money aboard, which was of course worthless, but we also found $500 in gold and greenbacks: jewelry, which we afterward sold for $750, and a number of knickknacks valuable as keepsakes. She was also a valuable prize for the Government as we found in her shallow hold two bales of cotton, about twenty muskets and carbines, and a lot of medical stores. It turned out that they were a bad gang, most of them being deserters, and in their operations along the coast they showed no partiality. The one who was wounded in the foot was an outlaw who was wanted for several murders and robberies, and was either hung or shot at Beaufort. The others were sent to prison for long terms, and thus the entire gang was wiped out.

Seventeen years after the close of the war I was at Bucksville, SC, and happened to be wearing a gold ring which was part of the plunder found on the sloop. The ring was identified by a gentleman named E.A. Haynes as one stolen from him in 1864, and was of course cheerfully handed over.

After the end of the war and with Reconstruction and the enforcement of the Emancipation Proclamation in effect, freed slaves were no longer part of the estates of the rice planters, whose wealth had been based on the work and value of their slaves. Only five years previously, the rice planters had been the wealthiest aristocrats in America, but now some were too poor to pay the taxes on their land. Some planters had fought and died in the war or escaped the South, never to return. Others returned to their ruined plantations and tried to start over. The planting of rice continued along Waccamaw Neck on a much smaller scale and had ceased altogether by the beginning of the twentieth century. A few of the emancipated slaves of Lowcountry plantations left South Carolina to find homes and jobs in other parts of the United States. Many of the ones who stayed refused to sign labor contracts with their former masters to work in the rice fields for the extremely low wages that were offered. They looked for other types of work or subsistence farmed and didn't hire themselves out at all. The business of planting rice in Lowcountry South Carolina failed because of the end of slavery, a series of hurricanes that caused water to top the rice field dikes and competition from rice producers in other states like Louisiana, Arkansas and Texas, where the soil would support machinery rather than require manual labor, as was necessary because of the soft mud in the Lowcountry.

There were no more summer vacations on North Island by aristocratic planters and their families accompanied by house slaves. Lafayette Village had fewer and poorer residents, all of whom had to take care of their own needs. They could still enjoy the sea breezes and good fishing at North Inlet. It is probable that at least a few former house slaves remembered how good the fishing had been at North Inlet and revisited Lafayette Village in their own boats or as employees of some of the homeowners who continued to live on North Island in the summer. However, over the years, the houses of Lafayette Village slowly deteriorated and were eventually washed away by more recent storms like the Hurricane of 1893, Hurricane Hazel in 1954 and Hurricane Hugo in 1989, all of which submerged North Inlet and other parts of the island. The shorelines at North Inlet have shifted and eroded, hiding any remnants of Lafayette Village that might have been found.

Without slaves to row their boats and tend their houses, white vacationers looked for summer homes at places that could be accessed more easily, such as Pawleys Island, a few miles north of North Island. Pawleys Island had also been a summer vacation destination for some planters. After the Civil War, a causeway was built across the marsh to connect four-mile-long Pawleys Island to the mainland. Pawleys Island was eventually divided into narrow oceanfront lots, which were sold for modest prices to white owners from all over South Carolina. More and more summer homes were built until, by the end of the twentieth century, there were almost four hundred houses on the island. If North Island had been as accessible by road as Pawleys Island, it might have been developed in the same way.

In 1867, the permanent lighthouse on North Island, which was built in 1811, was repaired and extended in height to eighty-seven feet. A new fifth-order Fresnel lens was installed, which could be seen from a distance of fourteen miles. Fuel for the lanterns changed from whale oil to lard to kerosene. A good and substantial two-story-and-attic frame dwelling was built, being in plan twenty-four by twenty-six feet, with a kitchen ten by ten feet and a porch extending along the entire front. A cistern was built and a boathouse on the beach. Lighthouse keepers George Durant and J.F. Anderson lived in the new house and took care of the lighthouse. The same year, the ninety-foot brig *Crocus* ran aground at North Island and was heavily damaged. The brig was sold at auction, recovered and rebuilt under the name of *Georgie*.

In 1874, keeper Anderson discovered the brig *Harry* drifting off the coast without a captain or navigator. He brought the brig to the quarantine station on South Island. The brig had been sailing toward Havana when the captain died of yellow fever, and two of the crewmen were ill with the same disease. A health officer visited the *Harry*; it was thoroughly fumigated and another captain assigned to take charge. Usually there was little to do at the quarantine station because visits to Georgetown from foreign ports were infrequent. In fact, foreign and domestic commerce was slower than before the war.

In 1875, the largest wooden sailing ship ever built in South Carolina, the *Henrietta*, which was constructed a few miles up the Waccamaw River at Bucksville, made its way with difficulty through Winyah Bay, passing close to the lighthouse on North Island. The three-masted ship, a Down-easter, was two hundred feet long, 1,200 tons and drew thirteen feet empty. To get over the shallow bar and into the ocean, it was raised up on a raft of two hundred empty turpentine barrels and towed out by a steam tugboat. Its masts and rigging were lying on deck. The tugboat towed the *Henrietta* to Charleston, where its masts, rigging and sails were installed. The *Henrietta* sailed from Charleston to Canada and thence all over the world, never returning to South Carolina. The ship wrecked in Japan in 1893, and its South Carolina longleaf pine planking, live oak frames and cypress trim were cut into small pieces and sold to the citizens of Japan for firewood.

JETTIES, WRECKS AND A LUMBER BOOM

The shifting outer bar at Winyah Bay continued to be treacherous for vessels going to and from Georgetown. In 1876, the thirty-two-ton schooner *Albion* was stranded on the bar and was a total loss. In 1879, the merchant steamer *National*, loaded with naval stores, encountered a heavy blow and high seas and foundered off the Winyah Bay bar. The vessel and cargo were lost, as were three of the seven-man crew. In January 1886, an article in the *Georgetown Enquirer* stated:

> The Schr Palmetto *from South Santee, with a cargo of nine hundred and sixty bushels of rough rice shipped by Col. Rutledge and consigned to Mssrs Baum Marks & Co. sank in Muddy Bay on Tuesday, the 12th inst. She was literally cut open by the ice-drifts. Her crew escaped in the boat and went over to North Island for shelter from the cold. The vessel and cargo are a total loss.*

These and other casualties revived efforts by the citizens of Georgetown to seek Federal funds to improve the entrance into Winyah Bay by building a stone jetty at the south end of North Island. A survey of the Georgetown Harbor entrance, made by the U.S. Army Engineers, revealed that at low tide there was only nine feet of depth over the bar. U.S. Army Engineers captain James Mercur recommended that the only solution to opening and maintaining a channel depth of eighteen feet would be a jetty system similar to the one being constructed at Charleston Harbor. In 1883, Congress approved funds for improving the rivers above Georgetown, but because of the huge expense involved, it did not approve monies for improving the Winyah Bay entrance. In 1896, the schooner *Alice J. Crabtree*, bound to New York with a cargo of logwood, was spoke off the Winyah Bay bar. It was out of provisions and had lost its main boom. Its captain wished to have his vessel towed into the harbor for repairs and replenishment of stores, but as it was drawing twelve and a half feet, the vessel was compelled to go to Charleston. In 1897, the schooner *Edgar C. Ross*, bound for New York, while being towed to sea, grounded on the bar. It was hauled off again, but not until half of its cargo had been thrown overboard and the vessel towed back to Georgetown.

In August 1885, a hurricane that struck near North Island destroyed the house where the pilots stayed, and they took refuge in the lighthouse. The newspaper noted, "The Lighthouse was in demand as a safe place of refuge."

The following was reported concerning the North Island lighthouse keeper, Daniel J. Knight, at 9:57 p.m. on August 31, 1886:

> *He was upstairs in bed when he heard a sound and felt a shock coming from eastward. He heard a noise as of thunder and jumped from his bed to the window, thinking it was a storm, but there was not a breath of wind. What he thought was thunder was a noise under ground, and before he had time to take a second thought the house was shaking. He felt eight or more shocks, but the first was the severest. He thought the shock strong, like a tremor, and the movement was vertical. His clock stopped at 9:57 p.m. It hung on the wall facing south. The pendulum is 2 feet long. The night was very calm and hot. The arches were shaken off the chimney on his cottage and the center plate and bolt of the lens in the tower were started. The tremor seemed to be east and west.*

What Mr. Knight had experienced was a shock from the earthquake that destroyed much of Charleston, sixty miles away. The keeper felt aftershocks from the quake as late as October 23, 1886.

One business that would be highly illegal today was tried on North Island in 1888. A commercial porpoise fishing business on North Island was initiated. An article in the *Georgetown Semi-Weekly Times* stated:

> *The large net to be used in the business has been completed, and materials have been sent to North Island for the erection of the necessary sheds and apparatus. The work of extracting the oil and preparing the skins for market*

A beached whale on North Island. *Courtesy of the Georgetown County Digital Library.*

> *will be done at the establishment on North Island. A crew of twenty-two hands will be employed in catching the fish and subsequently manipulating the blubber and hides. The net is a mammoth affair, consisting of three sections, whose combined length is one mile, with a depth of forty-five feet. The equipment includes a machine for splitting the hides. These are worth $2.50 apiece in the market today.*

The business was eventually abandoned.

Beginning in the early 1880s, commercial shipping of lumber to the Northeast from Georgetown and from sawmills along the rivers above Georgetown increased dramatically. These increases in use of the harbor entrance put additional pressure on the federal government to improve the entrance. Loaded schooners were being delayed for days, waiting for high tides sufficient to cross the bar. The Clyde Steamship Line refused to consider Georgetown as a port of call until the condition of the bar was improved. Throughout the 1880s, politicians and influential citizens from all over South Carolina lobbied Congress to provide funds for a jetty system for the Winyah Bay entrance. The estimated cost of the jetty system was $2.5 million. Finally, in 1890, Congress and the Board of Engineers approved some funds for the North Jetty, and work was started at the southern tip of North Island in 1891.

A schooner from New York unloading stones for the North Island jetty. *Courtesy of the Georgetown County Digital Library.*

The work inched along, and after a year, by June 30, 1892, the jetty, which was initially built to eighteen inches above the low-water mark, had been extended only 2,090 feet into the sea. Progress was slow because of the magnitude of the job. First, before the stone for the jetty could be placed on the ocean floor, large mattresses, woven of small saplings, had to be fixed to the bottom by stone ballast to provide a foundation for the stone. The mattresses for the project were made on the banks of the Sampit River near Georgetown and then towed to the jetty site. The stones could then be dumped into the water without having them sink into the sand. The report on the jetty work done in 1891–92 described the method of construction:

> *A part of the stone was brought by railroad from Columbia, S.C., and a part of it by schooner from New York. The latter was delivered from the vessel into tram cars at the contractor's wharf on North Island and dumped from them upon the jetty from a tramway built on piles driven along the harbor side of its axis. The stone from Columbia was towed on scows from Georgetown (12 miles) and delivered from the scows directly upon the jetty.*

Work on the much longer south jetty on South Island was also started in 1892. Work proceeded on both jetties throughout the 1890s, as Congress slowly appropriated funds for the work. The north jetty was completed in 1903 after reaching its ultimate length of 11,139 feet, with a crest of $4\frac{1}{2}$ to 6 feet above low water. To celebrate completion of the north jetty, a boat parade of surveyors and their queen motored from the jetty, through Winyah Bay, up the Sampit River and along the waterfront of Georgetown. The

The 1903 celebration of the completion of North Jetty by surveyors and their queen. *Courtesy of the Georgetown County Digital Library.*

North Jetty with shrimp boats at sunrise. *Photograph by Phil Wilkinson.*

south jetty was 21,051 feet long. Both jetties had been completed by 1905, at a total cost of $2,400,000. The *Winyah Bay*, a seagoing dredge called a sand sucker, which was over 100 feet long and could remove two thousand cubic yards of sand per day, was built and placed in service in 1898 to assist in obtaining the desired depth of channel: 15 feet at low water.

The south end of North Island was a very busy place during the 1890s. While the jetties were being built, the lumber industry of coastal South Carolina continued to increase in scope. Lumber barons of the Northeast and Midwest, having exhausted the forests of their regions, were moving into Georgetown and establishing large sawmills to transport longleaf pine and bald cypress lumber, along with naval stores, cut from forests as far away as one hundred miles by ship to booming cities in the North. Steamships, carrying over 1 million feet of lumber, and four-masted topsail schooners, carrying up to 600,000 feet, sailed in and out of Georgetown by day and night. Multiple steam tugboats towed sailing vessels through Winyah Bay. Citizens complained in newspaper editorials about unnecessary noise from the whistles of steamboats and tugboats at night. Several port pilots, both white and black, guided vessels up and down the intricate channel between Georgetown and the Atlantic Ocean. In 1895, more lighted markers were added to the channel between Georgetown and North Island. In 1898, a spar 32 feet long with proper halyards and lashings was rigged horizontally on the watch room gallery of the lighthouse, and a set of nineteen international code flags with marine glasses and signal books was supplied to the keeper. In 1899, a telephone line was installed to connect the station through South Island to Georgetown. The telephone number listed in Mouzon's telephone exchange directory for the lighthouse was 18.

On July 14, 1899, a letter to the editor of the *Georgetown Times* stated:

> *I saw a sight on our bar on Thursday morning that I know will interest most of our citizens. There could be seen on Winyah bar, between the hours of 9 and 11 o'clock, July 13, the Clyde steamship* Geo. W. Clyde; *tugs* Martha Helen, W.P. Congdon, S.S. Brewster, *and a Wilmington tug; one stern wheel steamer; steamer* Planter; *steamer* Merchant; *dredge* Winyah Bay; *three large 3-masted schooners; three jetty barges; two naptha launches; one pilot boat; and numerous small fishing craft. Almost all of these were to be seen at one time, and the show would have been credible for the entrance to New York City.*

Before 1900, a long and wide pier had been built on the Winyah Bay side of the lighthouse. Numerous excursions to North Island beach were sponsored by churches, the Sons of the Confederacy, the Woman's Christian Temperance Union and other organizations. On May 14, 1896, the *Columbia State* newspaper ran the following article:

> *Georgetown's Firemen*
> *A Delightful Excursion to North Island Given by Them*
> *Georgetown, May 14—Aboard the schooner* Warren B. Potter *the members of the Winyah Fire company yesterday gave their friends of Georgetown a most delightful excursion to North Island, distant about 12 miles from the City on the Sampit. The excursion is one of the annual events of Georgetown and no one ever fails to attend. The second trip was scheduled to leave at 6 o'clock, but the people continued to arrive in such numbers that it was well after that hour before the tug* Congdon *started down the river and out into the open bay with the* Warren B. Potter *in tow.*
>
> *On the schooner all was life and merriment. The band played and the young folk danced to the music. Young America ran riot and played hide and seek from the very bottom of the schooner.*
>
> *On the way out refreshments of a substantial nature were served and the salt breeze only added to the zest in disposing of them. Soon after 9 o'clock, North Island was reached. Here the young people broke up into twos and at convenient distances walked along the hard sandy beach. The moon shone bright and the night was such as lovers love. And judging from the interchange of tender looks, when the whistle of the* Congdon *the recall, there were not a few of them.*
>
> *The return was not less pleasant than the outgoing trip. Again dancing and refreshments kept all engaged until Georgetown was reached after 1 o'clock in the morning. The entire affair was most enjoyable.*

In 1901, the tug *Congdon* took forty Georgetonians out Winyah Bay to North Island for an excursion and to see the progress of jetty construction. A letter to the editor of the *Georgetown Times* reported:

> *At this stage of the proceedings the ladies came to the front, and in exactly 20 minutes they had spread a dinner that would have done justice to Delmonico or the Georgetown Rifle Guards. The substantials dispatched, (and we did think of ye Editor as the last lemon pie disappeared), we were informed that we could "do as we choose" and for the next two hours fishing, floating, flirting and frolicking were the order of the day.*

A party went up to see our old friend, Mr. Rowlinski, the lighthouse keeper, and came back bubbling over with enthusiasm equally as much for the keeper as for the lighthouse through which he had so courteously shown them.

Capt S.E. Woodbury (who had been captain of the Georgetown schooner Linah C. Kaminski *in 1885), an old deep sea mariner, was with us and he was constantly giving expressions to his admiration of the changes which have occurred on the bar since he gave up a sailor's life—about eight years ago. Then he had to wait inside the bar for weeks at a time occasionally to sail his vessel out on the high water, drawing 11 feet; while now it is a common thing for a vessel drawing sixteen feet to go out at an average high water.*

As the lumber boom progressed, the people of Georgetown prospered and took more excursions and vacations on North Island and Pawleys Island. The steamboats *General Safford*, the *Romain* and, later, the *Comanche*; the steam tugboats *Martha Helen* and *Congdon*; and the launch *Mary A* took numerous parties of excursionists from Georgetown to the pier at North Island, near the lighthouse. In 1913, a dance pavilion was completed at the

A dance pavilion was built on North Island in 1913. *Courtesy of the Georgetown County Digital Library.*

The steamboat *Comanche* made excursions to North Island. *Courtesy of the Pawleys Island Civic Association.*

base of the pier leading to the lighthouse from the Winyah Bay side, which made excursions even more popular.

In 1900, Atlantic Coast Lumber (ACL) bought property along Georgetown's waterfront and built the largest lumber mill east of the Mississippi River. Once the channel had been deepened to fifteen feet, ACL bought two large steamships, the *Waccamaw* and the *Georgetown*, each of which could transport over one million feet of lumber. It also leased a new four-masted schooner, the *City of Georgetown*, which was built in Bath, Maine, in 1902. In 1905, Georgetown celebrated its 100th year of incorporation with parades and speeches, including a boat and ship parade of fifty vessels with two U.S. Navy monitor vessels, the *Nevada* and the *Arkansas*, which were the first U.S. Navy vessels to enter Winyah Bay since the end of the Civil War. By the mid-1920s, the pine forests within one hundred miles of Georgetown had been cut down and not replanted. By the beginning of the Great Depression, ACL and several other big lumber companies had closed their doors. Georgetown and its port were left without an industry, and ship traffic dropped to almost nothing. It wasn't until after 1937 that the International Paper Company completed a huge pulp and paper mill in Georgetown and began to import some raw materials and ship some paper abroad.

A man, possibly the North Island Lighthouse keeper, and his wife, 1911. *Courtesy of the Georgetown County Digital Library.*

During the early 1900s, there were reports from lighthouse keepers and others about various incidents that occurred on or near North Island. In 1903, "the schooner *Minnehaha*, from Charleston, loaded with coal, sank near North Island on Friday last, the vessel and cargo proving a total loss. The coal was intended for the Government."

In 1909, a dwelling was built on South Island for the keeper, who was responsible for navigation markers on that side of Winyah Bay. In 1915, the keeper, who was living in the South Island house, committed suicide. The next year, 1916, it was decided to relocate the South Island house to North Island to consolidate the two keepers' houses. The feat of moving the house across Winyah Bay was described in the *Lighthouse Service Bulletin*:

> *The frame dwelling, 51 by 56 feet in plan, one and one-half stories high, weighing 115 tons, was rolled 500 feet on skids to a trestle out in the water arranged to span two lighters. Hand-power cotton screws were used*

North Island Lighthouse and keepers' houses. *Courtesy of the Georgetown County Digital Library.*

North Island Lighthouse and the Winyah Bay beachfront, 1919. *Courtesy of the Georgetown County Digital Library.*

to force the dwelling along. The lighters were placed in position at ebb tide, and at flood tide the building was lifted clear of the trestle and was towed across the bay by the tenders Snowdrop *and* Water Lily *to a similar trestle on the North Island side, the tender* Mangrove *assisting. From this point the dwelling was rolled 400 feet to the new site on the Georgetown reservation. The keeper's family occupied the dwelling during the operation. The kitchen was brought over separately in the same manner, and neither structure suffered any damage.*

In 1912, a *Daily Item* reporter related the experience of a local fisherman:

> *About 5 o'clock PM on Wednesday the 21ˢᵗ, myself and helper were lying by our shad net off North Island, I noticed that the wind which was from the southwest, was becoming much stronger, I concluded to take in my net and make for a harbor, but before this could be accomplished it was blowing great guns, and with one-half of my net in the boat which I managed to haul in like a rope catching about 150 shad, when I was forced to cut the net in two in order to relieve the fearful strain on my boat, which was likely to have been swamped at any minute. After this had been done, I started up the engine and made for shore, but it was impossible to stem the tide and wind, so headed about and ran before the gale, hoping to ride it out. As near as I could judge next morning we were about 75 miles off the western coast, but the storm swept by and we then proceeded to pull for shore, as we had to preserve our gasoline for cooking shad.*

The reporter asked how he did this, and the fisherman replied:

> *After preparing a shad we put gasoline on it and set the same on fire, thus baking it nicely, though it was not so palatable, but a hungry man can go anything.*
>
> *It was a terrible experience; during the night of the storm it seemed that the Atlantic ocean would be turned upside down, so high were the foamed crest waves, and I can only add that through a kind Providence and a staunch little boat, we escaped a watery grave. Goodbye, Mr. Reporter, may you never have a similar experience, and dine on gasoline planked shad.*

In 1914, the *Times* reported:

> *Persistent northeast winds have played hob with the prospects of floating the houseboat* Lunaria, *which, on her maiden voyage, went on the North Island beach near the jetty one night some weeks ago. As a matter of fact, the vessel has begun to go to pieces under the merciless pounding of the high-water surf. A part of the superstructure is gone and the hull is showing the effects of the heavy seas.*

The owners of the wreck of the *Lunaria*, which at the time of the accident was called "a handsome new house boat," were Mr. C.L. Ford and Mr. T.W. Brightman.

In 1914, another wreck of a vessel at North Inlet was bought by Mssrs. Ford and Brightman to recover its machinery. The *Georgetown Times* described the demise of the menhaden fishing vessel *A.M. Hathaway*:

> *The steam fishing schooner* A.M. Hathaway, *217 tons, Capt. Luce, Greenport, N.Y., is hard ashore at North Inlet, Winyah Bay, and she will probably leave her bones there. She is broadside on the beach, drawing 11 feet and with a scant six feet around her at high spring tide.*
>
> *She is practically full of sand and pumps are clogged with sand and there is scarcely one chance in a hundred that she will ever float again.*
>
> *The* Hathaway, *in company with the steam fisherman* Susquehannah, *233 tons, of Wilmington, N.C., was following a great school of menhaden down the coast Wednesday morning. The* Hathaway *was drifting, in close to the beach; the* Susquehannah, *being heavier and deeper, was further out. A brisk wind and strong tide at North Inlet caught the* Hathaway *and sent her on the sands, before the crew knew what happened. The skipper and crew did not think seriously of the matter when the vessel struck as they expected to be able to back off without difficulty on the full of the tide.*
>
> *With engines working at full capacity the vessel not only failed to slide off the sand, but actually stuck harder. Capt. Luce sent to town for a tug. The tug* E.T. Williams, *Capt. Porter, went to the aid of the stranded vessel, and for an hour and a half pulled on her with the throttle wide open. But the* Hathaway *refused to budge. She had wallowed herself down into a nest of quicksand and there was no pulling her over the rim of it.*
>
> *The* Susquehannah, *being too deep to get within hawser reach of the* Hathaway, *could not pass a line. She remained anchored half a mile away while the* Williams *was straining at her hopeless task.*
>
> *The* Hathaway *carried a crew of 24. All were saved. The* Hathaway *is a wooden craft, and was built at Fall River in 1873.*

Parts of the wreck of the *Hathaway* were still visible from North Inlet until recently.

Sometime around 1914, a story was told about a North Island lighthouse keeper who lived alone in the house next to the lighthouse with his little daughter, Annie. On mornings, when the tide was rising and flowing into Winyah Bay, he often rowed his boat to Georgetown to buy supplies, accompanied by Annie. He would row back with the current on an outgoing tide, arriving before nightfall to light the oil lamp at the top of the lighthouse. Late one cloudy morning, he and Annie rowed the ten miles to town, bought their provisions and started back with the falling tide in the mid-afternoon. The weather had deteriorated and Winyah Bay was rough, but he rowed on, knowing that he must arrive at North Island and light the lantern before dark. An east wind opposed the outgoing current and blew harder. The waves became high and steep, and Annie held on to her father for safety. The little wooden skiff took water over the bow, which began to rise in the bilge under their feet. He was less than half a mile from the shore of North Island, but the boat was filling with water, and he knew he wouldn't make it. Just before his boat went down, he tied a line around Annie and fastened her to him so that he could swim with her on his back. He swam with all his might, finally losing consciousness just as he was washed up on the shore. Hours later, when he awoke, he felt to make sure that Annie was still strapped to his back. Much to his despair, he discovered that she was dead. His fair-haired Annie was gone.

The lighthouse keeper never recovered from that horrible event. The people of Georgetown, particularly those who were mariners, sympathized and took pity on the keeper, but to no avail. It was less than a month later when a fisherman headed out of Winyah Bay in his trawler to fish. As he was crossing the bar, he looked to the side and was shocked to see a little, fair-haired girl sitting on the railing and looking straight at him. She pointed toward Georgetown and said, "Go back." Then, she disappeared. He knew he had seen a ghost. He was so surprised that he turned his boat around and headed back. Before he reached the dock in Georgetown, a violent storm came out of nowhere, and he was lucky to be safely tied up before its full fury struck. No one believed his story, but it happened to others again and again, always just before the beginning of an unanticipated storm. The ghost of Fair-haired Annie continues to appear, even today.

In 1919, Keeper K.E. Fremser "rendered assistance to an aeroplane with six occupants."

In 1921, Keeper Joseph Grissillo reported that the schooner *Phoebe Crosby* had struck the south jetty. On October 24, it was reported that Merritt and Chapman divers had "examined schooner *Phoebe Crosby* ashore near south jetty and found planking badly stove in below water line. Vessel lies easy on sandy bottom: chances of saving vessel doubtful." A November 9 *Georgetown Times* article reported:

> The 4-masted schooner Phoebe Crosby, *which was driven on the rocks of the South Jetty, while entering Winyah Bay under sail some three weeks ago, will be abandoned by the owners. After a thorough examination of the condition of the vessel, it became evident that the cost of salvaging the vessel would be too*

A young girl who might have been fair-haired Annie in front of the North Island Lighthouse. *Courtesy of the Georgetown County Digital Library.*

> *great. The* Crosby *was a fine new vessel of 1700 tons burden and made this port many times in the lumber trade. She was chartered to take on a cargo from the Rankin-Tyson Lumber Company of this city and was returning light from Providence. It is understood that she was insured for about $60,000. Captain Smail, in explanation of the accident which proved fatal to his ship, states that a sudden squall caught his vessel, a swift cross current contributing, and she was swung hard against the rocks, her stern receiving such severe damage that she sank with only the stern and the cabin remaining above water. Joseph Grisillo, the light keeper, with the tender* Palmetto *under captain E.F. Redell, witnessed the catastrophe and rendered immediate assistance under circumstances requiring great courage and coolness. Grisillo afterwards stood by and, for days was the means of communication and transportation between the land and the distressed master and crew, who refused to leave the ship.*

The *Phoebe Crosby* had been built and launched in 1921 by Crosby Navigation Company of Richmond, Virginia. It was named after the owner's wife, Phoebe Crosby, a soprano who was launching her singing career at the same time. A year after the wreck, the U.S. Army Engineers Office in Charleston advertised: "Bids until Nov. 27 for removing the wreck of schooner *Phoebe Crosby*, further information on application." Ms. Phoebe Crosby continued her brilliant operatic career until 1951.

In 1929, the tug *Hoodless* from Philadelphia wrecked in fog on the south jetty.

In 1930, the *Times* reported:

> With the evident intent of landing a cargo of liquor at some convenient point in this county, the Dorothy Ashley, a 33-ton schooner, sailing under British registry, put into Georgetown harbor Friday night, only to be halted by the United States Coast Guard patrol boat No. 240, off North Island light. The vessel was immediately taken into custody, the consignment of 800 cases of fancy whiskey seized, and the crew placed under arrest.
>
> The vessel sailed boldly into Winyah bay with a great part of the cargo above deck. There was no pretence of hiding the stuff, and when the Ashley was boarded, the officers rounded up the complete cargo in little or no time. Papers turned over to the coast guard officers showed that the craft is of British registry, and that the whiskey was taken aboard in Bermuda.

In November 1930, another yacht was boarded inside of North Inlet by the same U.S. Coast Guard boat, and another one thousand cases of whiskey were confiscated.

In 1932, a schooner was found beached and burned on Debordieu Beach with seventy-five cases of whiskey still on board.

In 1934, the largest sailing vessel ever to pass by the North Island lighthouse, the *Hussar V*, motored through Winyah Bay to Georgetown and tied up opposite the Kaminski house on the Sampit River, where it stayed for over a year. It was a 358-foot, four-masted, steel-hulled barque that belonged to Edward Hutton, founder of E.F. Hutton. He was married to Marjorie Merriweather Post, heiress to the *Post* cereal fortune. The *Hussar V* was there to wait out the divorce proceedings of the couple. The divorce settlement awarded the vessel to Ms. Post, who immediately changed the name to *Sea Cloud*. Later, in 1935, she married her third husband, Joseph Davis. The newlyweds took their honeymoon in the West Indies on the *Sea Cloud* with sixteen Georgetown boys as part of the seventy-two-man crew. Later, Davis was appointed ambassador to Russia, and the *Sea Cloud* was sailed there to be a floating diplomatic palace. At the beginning of World War II, the *Sea Cloud* was loaned to the United States Coast Guard. On January 9, 1942, the *Sea Cloud* sailed from Georgetown, where it had been moored for two years, to Baltimore, where it was refitted for war service. The masts were removed, it was armed and painted gray and it patrolled the waters off the East Coast of the United States and Canada. At the end of the war, it reverted to Marjorie Merriweather Post. It was given a facelift and sold to Dominican Republic dictator Rafael Trujillo. When Trujillo was assassinated in 1961, the *Sea Cloud* was bought by German businessmen, who converted it into a luxury cruise ship for the Caribbean and Mediterranean.

In 1938, the assistant North Island Lighthouse keeper was drowned and the chief keeper injured in an explosion aboard their twenty-five-foot lighthouse boat while en route from Georgetown to North Island

The North Island Lighthouse was manned by resident lighthouse keepers from the U.S. Lighthouse Service from the beginning of its operation in 1812 until after World War II. In 1939, President Roosevelt merged the U.S. Lighthouse Service into the United States Coast Guard (USCG). During World War II, as many as eleven coast guardsmen boarded with the civilian lighthouse keepers and their families on North Island, and others lived in tents as they patrolled the beaches on horseback and manned a weather station. When the last of the civilian keepers retired in 1947, one of the keeper's houses was modified to serve as a barracks for the coast guardsmen who operated the lighthouse. In 1968, a fire destroyed the two original keepers' houses. The USCG built masonry block buildings to house its personnel.

In 1984, the *Charleston News & Courier* reported that the North Island Lighthouse would be automated soon and described the then-present duties of the USCG:

> *Today the work involves mostly maintenance and sending periodic weather reports on ocean conditions, and monitoring numerous buoys, 165 light ranges and other guideposts from Little River Inlet near the North Carolina line to Breach Inlet outside Charleston. The facility also provides dockside services for boaters who run out of gas or provisions, and the crew serves as a backup unit to the Winyah Rescue squad. At times it is involved in raids against drug and illegal smuggling.*

In 1986, the light was automated, and it was no longer necessary to have a USCG keeper at the lighthouse.

In 1988, the South Carolina Department of Juvenile Justice leased the property around the lighthouse and the buildings that the USCG had built to the Associated Marine Institute (AMI). Adolescent offenders and their instructors lived and went to school on the island. One of the teachers at AMI on North Island at that time was Jane, a petite New England lady in her fifties. She said that there were about twenty male kids living on the island. She would leave her home in Georgetown early each morning, arrive at the pier along the Sampit River, make sure that the food and supplies that had been delivered to the boat were of the correct quantity, board the cabin boat, ride through Winyah Bay for ten miles to a pier near the lighthouse, climb the ladder to the pier (when she was interviewed for her job, she was asked to climb the ladder; she did so and then was told that the last applicant had fallen from the ladder and been turned down for the job), greet the twenty boys between the ages of thirteen and seventeen, teach them all subjects all day until 4:00 p.m., climb down the ladder and ride the boat back to Georgetown, accompanied by the day's accumulated trash. There were minders at the school, day and night, who looked after security and kept order. The kids who were there were classified by the South Carolina Juvenile Justice System as adjudicated youth who were earning their way back into society.

Jane said that one of the problems was the roughness of Winyah Bay during bad weather. On one occasion, she was leaving North Island as a gale was brewing. Another large male teacher with diabetes was the only other passenger as the boat captain prepared to return to Georgetown. The boat was rising and falling several feet with the waves. She helped the diabetic down the ladder, and he kneeled in the bottom of the boat, praying for deliverance. Jane was told to go to the plunging bow, disconnect the mooring line and "Hold on!" When she released the bowline, the boat roared forward to clear the pier as Jane held on for dear life. When they had smashed and crashed their way back to Georgetown, she asked the captain what time they would be going back in the morning. He said, "Little lady, you won't be going back out there for at least three more days in this weather." Finally, about 1993, the school found another location on the mainland, and because of the inconveniences of supplying food, drinking water, healthcare and other services to the island, it abandoned North Island.

In 2001, the USCG deeded the lighthouse property to the South Carolina Department of Natural Resources, and it became part of the Tom Yawkey Wildlife Center. North Island Lighthouse remains sturdy and well back from the water. It is the oldest lighthouse still in operation in South Carolina and is one of the oldest in the United States. The fifth-order Fresnel lens, manufactured in 1869 in Paris, France, by Sautter, Lemonnier & Cie and installed in the Georgetown Lighthouse in 1870, stayed in use until 1986. The lens is now displayed in the South Carolina Maritime Museum in Georgetown. The present automated light and equipment in the lighthouse are maintained by coast guardsmen from their station in Georgetown. Its white light flashes twice every fifteen seconds.

WEALTHY OWNERS OF
NORTH ISLAND

North Island is shown on some eighteenth-century maps as Cravens Island. William, Earl of Craven, was one of the Lords Proprietors who had authority from the king until 1729 to grant large tracts of land to settlers. Huguenot Paul Trapier was an agent for the Lords Proprietors and first owner of Cravens, or North Island. He was succeeded by a son, Paul Trapier, born in 1716, who became a wealthy Georgetown merchant and was known as the "king of Georgetown." His descendents owned much of North Island well into the nineteenth century, until it was sold to Thomas Hume. Thomas M. Hume, whose family also owned a rice plantation across Winyah Bay on Cat Island, advertised North Island for sale at auction in 1850. The advertisement read:

> *That well known island at the mouth of Winyah Bay, called NORTH ISLAND, and containing between 12 and 13,000 acres of land, the greater part of it is well wooded and a portion is admirably adapted to the culture of long staple Cotton. For a number of years past, this island has been a place of resort during the summer months, for most of the planters on the neighboring rivers, and has acquired a great reputation for health, etc.*

In 1869, North Island was owned by John Bavsketh. In 1884, because of unpaid taxes, a sheriff's sale occurred. Ten thousand acres, which included North Island, South Island and part of Cat Island, were bought by retired Civil War general E.P. Alexander, who had first visited the islands during the early 1880s to hunt and fish. Edward Porter Alexander was born in Georgia in 1835, the son of a wealthy plantation owner. He graduated from West Point in 1857 and served in the U.S. Army until the beginning of the Civil War. He joined the Confederate army as a captain of engineers in 1861. By the end of that year, he had been promoted to lieutenant colonel. He served with distinction throughout the war, rising to the rank of general.

His most famous engagement was on July 3, 1863, at the Battle of Gettysburg, during which he was in command of all artillery for General Longstreet's corps. He started the day that General Robert E. Lee and the South lost the war by conducting a massive two-hour bombardment of Union positions on Cemetery Ridge, using over 150 guns. When the bombardment was stopped because of a shortage of ammunition, it was realized that it hadn't been as effective as needed. Colonel Alexander gave the order for Pickett's Charge, which failed, and by the end of the day, the battle was lost. At the end of the war, General Alexander was with General Robert E. Lee at Appomattox Court House, where he gave Lee advice—which wasn't taken—to continue the conflict as a guerrilla war. After the war, he was a professor of mathematics at the University of South Carolina in Columbia for a short time. He became an executive and president of several railroads, including the Louisville & Nashville Railroad. It was during this time that he first began to hunt and fish on North Island.

In 1884, a curious article appeared in the *Georgetown Enquirer*:

Gen. E.P. Alexander, the distinguished railroad president, has recently been on a visit to Georgetown County. On his return to Augusta he has sent Col. Butler, our State fish commissioner, a fish the likes of which no expert in the office has ever seen. The fish is thirty-nine inches long, seven inches in girth, and weighs only one pound. It has no scales, and no fins except the dorsal and the pectoral. The dorsal fin is large and extends along the entire backbone. The tail is long and ends in a keen point like the tip of a whip, there being no fin at the extremity. The head is large and savage looking. The eyes are likewise large, measuring an inch across. The teeth are very long and sharp, and those on the tip of the under jaw project in front of the end of the upper jaw. The fish is evidently rapacious. Gen. Alexander, in his letter to Col. Butler, says he found it on the beach of North Island, Winyah Bay, on Friday last, and as it was quite out of the common run. He sent it to our State fish commissioner, requesting that its name be sent him if that could be ascertained. The fish was entirely new to all the natives who saw it except the lighthouse-keeper, (an old sailor) who said that he had once seen such a fish caught in mid-ocean by a line trolling from a steamer. Gen. Alexander adds that he is about starting a sturgeon and possibly a menhaden fishery on North Island, and will be in

Georgetown County most of the spring. The fish is a very interesting specimen and Col. Butler will endeavor to have it identified.

This fish remained unidentified.

General Alexander built houses on both South Island and North Island. A personal column in the *Georgetown Enquirer* in 1886 said, "General E.P. Alexander spent the holidays at his castle on North Island." President Grover Cleveland, a friend of General Alexander, visited him several times to go duck hunting, shooting hundreds of ducks each time. In 1897, President Cleveland appointed Alexander as arbiter of a commission to set a boundary between Nicaragua and Costa Rica, with the idea of the United States building a canal across Central America. Alexander lived in Nicaragua until 1899, when his wife, Bettie Mason Alexander, died.

The North Island property was in the name of his wife, and her will transferred North Island to her husband. The document that conveyed North Island to her husband described the property being transferred:

All that tract and parcel of land situate lying and being in said County of Georgetown State of South Carolina known as North Island including Collins Island and bounded as follows: on the north by North Inlet, on the east and south by the Atlantic Ocean on the west by Winyah Bay and Jones Creek back to point of departure containing six thousand acres more or less.

General E.P. Alexander remarried and retired to his home on South Island. He sold several lots on South Island, known as Fishermen's Village, and on North Island where a few houses were built. During his retirement, Porter Alexander wrote two major books about the war, which are considered by historians to be the most objective and sharpest resources written by a person involved in the Civil War. In 1902, Alexander was with President Theodore Roosevelt and General Longstreet on the podium at West Point's Alumni Day, where he delivered the most rousing speech of the day, praising Confederate soldiers for fighting for their home, acknowledging the "Lost Cause" and looking toward a bright future for the nation. Shortly before his death in 1910, Alexander attempted to sell his entire holdings, including North Island. The realtor circulated a description of North Island at that time. After extolling the duck and deer hunting opportunities on the island, the article read:

The future value of this island is sure to be very largely increased by the location upon it of the end of the Jetty. This was so secured that from the first the island

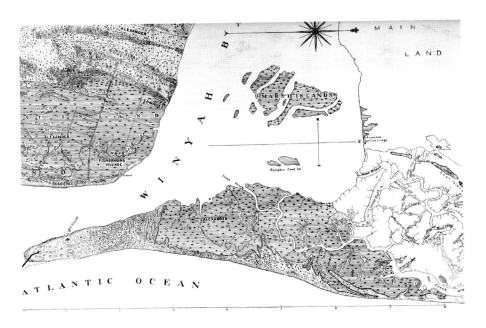

A 1907 map of North Island and South Island. *Courtesy of the South Carolina Department of Natural Resources.*

has begun to grow along the jetty, building, as it goes, beautiful beaches on both sides with every variety of water for either still or surf bathing. There need be no stagnant water within miles, and a magnificent site is already formed for a summer resort, on which the mosquito need be totally unknown.

The U.S. Government owns a site of 6 acres on North Island on which the Georgetown light-house is located and a coal shute for the use of the Harbor Dredge.

Deep water approaches the shore very closely below the Light-house, and only a short wharf will be needed to enable vessels to land. The distance to Georgetown is about 13 miles by water.

In addition to this opportunity to make a superb summer resort, sure to be soon demanded by the rapidly increasing population of Georgetown, an even greater commercial value will be found in the enormous sand hills running entirely across the island and far along the front beach, as a site for a Sand-brick or Concrete Factory, to which schooners could deliver Cement, Lime and Coal and from which they could freight, without drayage, the products to any port on the Atlantic, Gulf or Caribbean Coast. The mild and healthful climate would permit work during every month of the year. There is no scarcity of sand

*along the Atlantic Coast but there is a scarcity of deepwater harbors in close
proximity to such immense accumulations of it. All sites where seagoing vessels
can approach land have great and growing industrial value for the location of
manufacturing enterprises of many kinds requiring ample room.*

The buyer of North Island was J.L. Wheeler, a Michigan millionaire lumber
and mining industrialist who had moved to Marion, South Carolina, at the
beginning of the twentieth century. He bought eight thousand acres of North
Island from General Alexander in 1909. He and partner Richard Cartwright
started the North Island Club and sold shares to those who wanted to hunt and
fish on North Island. Wheeler visited North Island many times and kept his
motor yacht, *Temiskaming*, available to take visitors to the island.

When General Alexander died in 1910, twenty thousand acres of his
land in Georgetown County, including South Island and part of Cat
Island, were bought for hunting and fishing purposes by Detroit playboy
Bill Yawkey, son of deceased lumber tycoon William Yawkey, who had
been the richest man in Michigan. Bill Yawkey had inherited ownership of
the Detroit Tigers baseball team from his father and enjoyed entertaining
some of Detroit's baseball players at South Island, including the famous
Ty Cobb. Bill Yawkey joined Wheeler's North Island Club and eventually
bought North Island from Wheeler and Cartwright.

In 1903, Bill adopted his nephew Tom Yawkey, whose father died soon
after Tom was born. When Bill Yawkey died in 1918, his estate left sixteen-
year-old Tom with a fortune of $7 million and most of his property in
South Carolina when Tom reached his thirtieth birthday. Bill Yawkey's wife,
Margaret, inherited North Island. Tom graduated from Yale and lived a life
of leisure during the Roaring Twenties. He married Alabama beauty queen
Elise Sparrow. When he reached his thirtieth birthday in 1933 and received
his inheritance, he bought the Boston Red Sox baseball team. Tom Yawkey
also bought North Island from Margaret Yawkey.

Tom Yawkey loved to hunt and fish in South Carolina, whereas his wife
loved the social whirl of New York and Boston. They were divorced in 1944.
Yawkey soon married Jean Hiller, who enjoyed a quieter life and loved
baseball. They split their time between summers in Boston, watching the
Red Sox, and winters at South Island. On a few occasions during the next
several years, he invited retired Red Sox players, including Ted Williams, to
visit his South Island plantation.

Yawkey is remembered for some things that had nothing to do with North
Island. He was known and criticized as someone who never had to work a

day in his life. He was criticized for delaying as long as possible the hiring of black players for the Red Sox baseball team. In 1936, Tom Yawkey participated in the "Bordello Project," loaning money to a madam to set up a house of prostitution, Sunset Lodge, just outside Georgetown for the benefit of construction workers building the huge International Paper Company mill. Sunset Lodge became notorious long after Yawkey had anything to do with it. Sunset Lodge was not the first bawdy house in Georgetown. In 1910, at the time of the lumber boom, when hundreds of sailors were on liberty in Georgetown, there were six bawdy houses listed in the census, with a total of twenty-three girls in residence. Sunset Lodge closed in the late 1960s.

Yawkey was a generous man who made philanthropic contributions to the Georgetown community. He financed the start-up of Tara Hall home for boys, and he gave money for healthcare facilities and other charities in Georgetown. Tom Yawkey was always friendly toward the people of Georgetown and to the coast guardsmen who lived on North Island. He occasionally hosted suppers for them at the employees' recreation hall on South Island. Yawkey dismantled a section of Dr. Alexander Hume's 1820 hunting lodge on Cat Island and moved it next to his house on South Island, using it to house his guests. When his original home on South Island burned in 1959, he never rebuilt. He and Jean put a house trailer next to the lodge and lived there for the remainder of the times they visited South Island.

Tom Yawkey built a rough hunting lodge on a small hummock of high land on North Island near Jones Creek, where he would bring guests in the winter to hunt black ducks and wild turkeys and eat delicious oysters gathered from the edge of the creeks. He also had an annual deer drive hunt on North Island. To navigate from South Island to the mouth of Jones Creek on North Island was tricky, especially at night, so Yawkey set tall posts with flambeaux to act as a range across Mud Bay to Jones Creek.

With the development of the outboard gasoline engine, more and more hunters and fishermen found it easier to trespass and poach on North Island land. Running motorboats through Jones Creek at high speeds was dangerous, and one boater was killed in a head-on collision. It was about that time that Yawkey began to discourage the public from coming onto his land without permission. Bud Caines lived on the island and acted as a watchman. After World War II, Yawkey had a palmetto log pier built into Winyah Bay from North Island, thinking he would log that end of the island, but his logger discovered that the trees were "wind shook" and not suitable for lumber, so he terminated the effort.

Phil Wilkinson and Tom Yawkey on South Island. *Courtesy of Phil Wilkinson.*

Phil Wilkinson, a noted wildlife biologist and photographer, was Tom Yawkey's superintendent advisor and confidant who lived on South Island with his family for many years. Phil was also a friend of Thomas Samworth, a wealthy publisher and owner of Dirleton and Exchange Plantations on the Pee Dee River. During Samworth's later years, he came to live with Phil Wilkinson's family on South Island, where he also became a friend of Tom Yawley. Samworth had previously given Dirleton Plantation to the South Carolina Wildlife Department (later to become the South Carolina Department of Natural Resources). Samworth probably influenced Tom Yawkey to donate his properties to the state. Thomas Yawkey was a conservationist, who spent millions of dollars to improve the waterfowl habitat on his properties. He impounded some of the marshes on South Island and Cat Island to become habitat for ducks, alligators and many species of birds. When Tom Yawkey died in 1976, he left his twenty-thousand-acre endowed estate in South Carolina to the South Carolina Department of Natural Resources, land that now composes the Tom Yawkey Wildlife Center. Consisting of Cat Island, South Island and most of North Island, the land is maintained as a wildlife preserve and nature center and was one of the largest conservation grants in U.S. history. North Island was designated as a wilderness area by Yawkey, to remain an undisturbed habitat for turtles, migratory birds, eagles and many other endangered species.

In 1888, Annandale Gun Club leased three thousand acres of marsh property behind North Island for twenty years for duck hunting. It was there, in 1894, that President Grover Cleveland became stuck in the marsh mud while duck hunting. He was freed by local guide Sawney Caines, but Caines became so appalled by President Cleveland's poor shooting that he shouted, "Sit down and gimme dat gun. Even if yo' is de Presi-dent of the Nunited States, yo' ain't worth a damn!" On another occasion, it was written that "Grover Cleveland picked up 58 ducks and lost 16."

The land that Annandale Gun Club leased was part of Hobcaw Barony, a seventeen-thousand-acre tract consisting of the far north end of North Island, North Inlet, a two-mile section of Debordieu Beach and the marshes and mainland forests west of North Island. Between 1905 and 1907, Bernard Baruch, who was born in Camden, South Carolina, and became a wealthy New York financier and statesman, bought all of Hobcaw Barony. Hobcaw Barony had been owned by the Alston family. Baruch used Hobcaw primarily as a retreat for hunting and fishing. When the existing house burned down in 1931, he built a new house on the property where he entertained such dignitaries as Winston Churchill, Franklin Roosevelt, Claire Booth Luce and others before and during World War II.

In April 1944, President Franklin D. Roosevelt was diagnosed by his closest doctors as having a serious heart disease and was in need of immediate rest. Although planning for the D-Day invasion of France was well underway, Roosevelt was told that he must get away from Washington if he wanted to live to run for a fourth term as president. President Roosevelt's friend and advisor Bernard Baruch quietly offered Hobcaw Barony as a place where the president could take his needed vacation. FDR stayed at Hobcaw for four weeks. The security precautions around Hobcaw were very strict, and the beaches of North Island were among those patrolled by the navy and coast

Belle Baruch, Bernard Baruch, Diana Churchill and Winston Churchill at Hobcaw in 1932. *Courtesy of the Belle W. Baruch Foundation.*

guard. During Roosevelt's stay, he was taken fishing in Winyah Bay and North Inlet. His stay at Hobcaw may have helped to add another year to his life.

During World War II, Bernard Baruch's daughter, Belle, who was born in 1899, helped the coast guardsmen patrol South Carolina beaches by patrolling her own beach at Debordieu and North Inlet. She was involved in at least one encounter with German agents trying to sneak ashore. In 1956, Bernard Baruch sold Hobcaw to Belle, who had been a world-famous horsewoman, flyer and sailor. For several years, she lived at Bellefield, the name she gave to her property. By the time of her death in 1964, she had created a foundation to manage the land as a conservation laboratory for the colleges and universities of South Carolina.

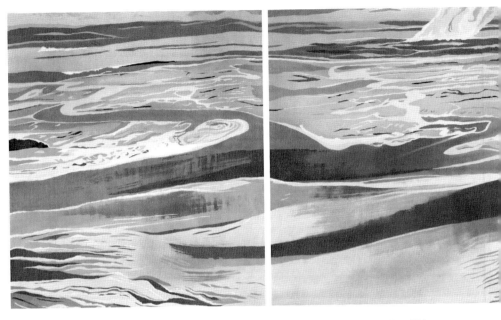

Hobcaw Barony (4' x 12'), a colorful batik on silk depicting North Inlet by artist Mary Edna Fraser, displayed at the Baruch Foundation. *Courtesy of Mary Edna Fraser.*

Hobcaw Barony includes North Inlet, which, in 1992, was designated the North Inlet–Winyah Bay National Estuarine Research Reserve. The reserve protects 18,900 acres of habitats, ranging from tidal and transitional marshes to oyster reefs, beaches and inter-tidal flats and from coastal island forests to open waterways. With more than 90 percent of North Inlet estuary's watershed in its natural forested state, its relatively untouched salt marshes and ocean-dominated tidal creeks have higher water and habitat quality than adjacent Winyah Bay. The reserve is home to many threatened and endangered species, including sea turtles, sturgeons, least terns and wood storks.

Two miles north of North Inlet is the now-developed part of Debordieu Beach, which extends north almost to Pawleys Island. It originally consisted of several Waccamaw River rice plantations, which extended from the Waccamaw River to the Atlantic Ocean. Most of these plantations were owned by the Alston, Allston or Ward families. After the Civil War, the various properties were held by family heirs who were not nearly so well off as before the war. Between 1906 and 1925, Dr. Issac Edward Emerson purchased several of these plantations.

Dr. Emerson, the son of a North Carolina farmer, graduated from the University of North Carolina, opened a drugstore in Baltimore in 1880 and eventually patented a formula for the headache medicine Bromo-Seltzer. He became extremely wealthy, lived a lavish lifestyle, owned several yachts and married twice. The daughter of his first wife, Margaret, married at age eighteen. She and her husband were social leaders in New York until Margaret filed a sensational divorce suit, claiming that her husband beat her in drunken rages. In 1911, Margaret was remarried to wealthy Alfred Vanderbilt, who died aboard the *Lusitania* in 1915. They had two sons, Alfred Jr. and George, born in 1914. Margaret inherited her husband's fortune and the fortune of Dr. Emerson, who died in 1931.

Eventually, Margaret's son George Vanderbilt inherited part of the Vanderbilt and Emerson fortunes and all of the South Carolina plantation properties that Dr. Emerson had owned. George married Louise Parsons, and they had one daughter, Lucille, in 1935. George was a yachting enthusiast who conducted scientific marine research all over the world between 1934 and 1941. He and Louise later divorced. He remarried in 1950 but divorced again in 1958. He lived part of his later life at his South Carolina plantation, Arcadia, on the Waccamaw River. He died in California in 1961. The plantations were inherited by his daughter, Lucille.

Lucille Vanderbilt was married to Wallace Pate and was living at Arcadia Plantation in 1970, when they made a decision to develop portions of their Debordieu property. During the next forty years, over 1,200 homesites were sold. Several are on the oceanfront toward the south end of the property, two miles from North Inlet. There have been occasional disputes between the property owners of Debordieu and the Baruch Foundation. The Debordieu homeowners wanted to dredge the channel of a natural creek leading from canals behind their homes toward North Inlet, but their request was denied. On another occasion, the homeowners wanted to construct groins near the south end of their property to counteract erosion of the beach, which was threatening to undermine several expensive beachfront homes. If construction of groins had been allowed, it might have trapped sand and caused erosion of the beach at North Inlet. The request was opposed and withdrawn.

During the 1970s and 1980s, North Inlet was a popular destination for houseboats and cruisers to gather for extended partying, barbecues on the beach, clam digging, fishing and baking in the sun. Annual Fourth of July celebrations were held, which included the crowning of a bogus "Mayor of North Inlet." Lilo, the artist wife of Georgetown resident Dickie Crayton, created a highly decorated mayor's crown. Families came on boats from Georgetown, Debordieu Beach and Pawleys Island for the annual long weekend event. The *Georgetown Times* described one such event in July 1976, the bicentennial year:

> *A dazzled Dickie Crayton, long-time habitué of Winyah Bay and points beyond and in between, donned the gorgeously hued gourd of authority, Saturday following a hot contest for the mayorship of the principality of North Inlet. The new mayor forthwith proclaimed North Inlet as one of the "greatest and most unspoiled areas along the Atlantic seaboard" and pledged to "keep it that way."*

Dickie Crayton, a recognized Georgetown individualist, owned the wooden houseboat *Casa Del Gato*, which had no engine, always leaked and had to be towed by his motorboat, *Homa Homa*.

The article went on to say, "In addition to a new mayor, North Inlet because of its increasing population and visitors, qualified for an increased council. This was in view of a Sunday census of around 500 people there." The annual July 4 weekend celebrations at North Inlet continued for some years but have died out in recent years.

A WILDERNESS FOR ALL TIMES

Tom Yawkey's will of 1976 stated:

> *The property known as North Island described above, shown on the map above mentioned constituting a part of this my will, shall be held and used for all time as a wilderness area without permanent structures or human habitation and without roads of any sort, temporary or permanent, except as may be necessary for the protection and management of the property and for the benefit of the fish and wildlife thereon. Access to such area may be permitted for scientific and educational purposes, and in the case of emergencies regarding the health of persons or damage to property, but no activities detrimental to its primitive wilderness character shall be permitted.*

A wide variety of wildlife lives on the beaches and in the marshes and forests of North Island. Deer, bobcats, raccoons, opossums, foxes, otters, minks, squirrels, rabbits, wild turkeys, rats, snakes and invasive wild hogs and coyotes live in the forests or at the edge of the marsh. Ducks and geese visit the island in winter. Over two hundred species of birds have been noted as permanent residents or transients. Bald eagles and other birds of prey nest in the trees of isolated North Island. The protected beaches of North Island and North Inlet provide sanctuary for ducks, pelicans, spoonbills, wood storks, ibis, loons and many other species of seabirds and shorebirds. Fiddler crabs in the marsh are captured by ibis to feed their young. Many

Nesting royal terns. *Photograph by Phil Wilkinson.*

hundreds of species of insects live their lives above or just under the ground of the island. North Island is the second densest sea turtle nesting beach in South Carolina. The marshes of North Inlet and its creeks nurture crabs, stone crabs, oysters, clams and other shellfish. Many of the creatures that thrive on North Island have been depleted or have disappeared from other coastal and river environments because of pollution or development. North Inlet and other nearby waters are ideal for over one hundred species of fish, including spawning shad and sturgeon. Alligators, which don't like to live in a saltwater environment, occasionally wander over to North Island from South Island and Cat Island. Each winter, feral hog hunts are held on North Island, sponsored by the South Carolina Department of Natural Resources. These hogs are descendents of those brought by the rice planters and are destructive to native plants, nesting birds and turtle nests. All structures that existed on North Island, except for those near the lighthouse, have disappeared. No humans live on North Island, but many visit for a short time to fish, collect shells or just enjoy the ocean breezes and beaches of an isolated island. A few commercial trawlers still drag their nets close to the shore of North Island to catch shrimp.

The shorelines of North Island and South Island were, and still are, affected by the rock jetties. The natural north–south shifts of the shoreline were impeded by construction of the jetties, causing accretion of portions of the shorelines of North Island and South Island. The global rise in sea level is contributing to erosion of some of the fragile beaches of North Island. Rising sea levels, along with a reduced flow of silted water from the dammed rivers feeding Winyah Bay, is causing some dieback of the cordgrass in the salt marshes behind North Island. Cordgrass has the richest and most important nutrients for all sea life, according to Dr. Dennis M. Allen, resident director of the Baruch Marine Field Laboratory. Smooth cordgrass, *Spartina alternaflora*, is one of the most remarkable plants on earth because of its ability to live and thrive in salt water. South Carolina has more area of salt marsh than any other Atlantic coast state. Protection of the salt

A good day's catch of channel bass at North Inlet. *Courtesy of the Georgetown County Digital Library, Tarbox Collection.*

marshes is essential to the survival of shellfish, fish and all of the birds and other creatures that depend on the marsh grasses for their food supply.

The long-term effects of natural and man-made changes in the physical, chemical and biological environment of North Inlet and the surrounding marshes are monitored by researchers and educators of the Belle W. Baruch Institute for Marine & Coastal Sciences, College of Arts & Sciences, University of South Carolina. North Inlet estuary has been the focus of much of the research conducted by the Baruch Institute since 1969. The mission of the institute is to conduct research and support education that will improve the management of marine and coastal resources and advance

The eroding beach along part of North Island. *Photograph by Phil Wilkinson.*

basic science for the well-being of people and the environment. The thirty permanent researchers and many visiting researchers and educators work from a modern twenty-five-thousand-square-foot complex of buildings at the edge of the marsh behind North Inlet. The North Inlet–Winyah Bay National Estuarine Research Reserve, sponsored by the National Oceanic and Atmospheric Administration (NOAA), funds much of the research by the University of South Carolina Marine Lab and Clemson University, which monitor on a long-term basis all flora, fauna and physical changes in the environment of North Inlet and surrounding marshes and forests and compare such things as water quality and growth of *Spartina* grasses in North Inlet versus Winyah Bay. Invasive species of plants and creatures are studied for their long-term effects on the environment. The many projects that have been undertaken and completed since 1969 have led to improvements in marine management and to a better understanding of how systems respond to global warming and other changes in the environment.

North Island's oceanfront beaches slope gently upward toward pine-covered dunes, which rise as much as fifty feet above the sea on parts of the island. The fine white quartz sand between the high and low tide marks, streaked with minerals from river sediments, is home to a multitude of tiny creatures that live just under the surface of the sand and are the target of

Ripples in the sand on the beach of North Island. *Photograph by Phil Wilkinson.*

birds feeding along the beach. Wave-carved ripple marks, gullies, pools and shell fragments wash in from the sea and leave their marks in the sand at low tide. It is rare to see a human footprint in the sand.

North Island is a matriarch, a tough old lady who has endured human contact for thousands of years. Native Americans visited her to hunt and fish and thought of her as their own until they were driven away by Europeans. Englishmen bought land along rivers near her and made fortunes by growing and selling rice. Planters came to her in summer to escape discomforts and diseases on their plantations. Negro slaves were brought to her to serve the needs of their masters. A lighthouse was built to guide ships past her. Hurricanes struck her, destroying homes and people. Soldiers built forts and patrolled her beaches. She was almost abandoned when Abraham Lincoln freed the slaves, defeated the slave owners and left planters in poverty. Thousands of ships passed by her, hauling lumber to the north. A stone jetty was built at her south end, adding land behind the stones. Ships wrecked against her jetty or grounded along her shore. Wealthy industrialists bought her marshes and beaches for hunting ducks and deer. Recent owners tried to think of ways to develop her, but she proved too remote and inaccessible. Finally, she was deserted by humans, protected against development and left to the changes that nature dictates.

North Island is fifty miles west of the Gulf Stream and is the southernmost land that touches Long Bay, that part of the Atlantic Ocean that stretches between the ocean inlets of Winyah Bay and Little River. Above North Inlet is the Grand Strand, comprising the developed beaches of Debordieu, Pawleys Island, Litchfield and all of the other developments south and north of Myrtle Beach, stretching well up into North Carolina.

North Island is the northernmost of a series of undeveloped and protected barrier islands. All of the shoreline of South Carolina, south of Debordieu Beach and stretching as far south as Capers Island, near Charleston, is protected from development. North Island, coupled with the Baruch Foundation's beaches at North Inlet and Debordieu, plus the rest of the Yawkey beaches at South Island and Cat Island, the Santee Delta and Cedar and Murphy Islands (donated by the Santee Gun Club), add up to twenty-five miles of protected shoreline. Joining Murphy Island at its southern end is an additional twenty-five miles of protected beach along the barrier islands of Cape Romain National Wildlife Refuge, which stretches almost to Charleston. This total of fifty miles of protected beach is the longest contiguous protected shoreline in the state

Deer in the surf at North Island. *Photograph by Phil Wilkinson.*

of South Carolina. In addition, there are many miles of protected rivers, swamps and forests that connect to Winyah Bay and the Santee Delta.

Occasionally, in winter, when the mosquitoes are gone, a small boat will approach high land at the back of North Island through a shallow creek and tie up. Its occupants walk and wade for half a mile beside the marsh and through a dense pine forest, passing a few ancient live oak trees and continuing toward the beach. They hear the distant sound of the surf and smell salt air before breaking out of the woods at the top of a dune and descending to the isolated beach. They look out to sea, watch the eternal rhythm of the waves and, perhaps, realize the true meaning of life.

The Keepers

Was there a village?

Before the village, tribes—
Santee, Waccamaw and Sampit—foraging in the wide salt marshes
leaving shards of evidence, arrowheads, one obsidian found
in the rutted sand at B'osin Point, suggesting trade from traveling
tribes—a midden of treasures. The first keepers, sea watchers
who fished the channel, crossed the wide bay from one barrier

island to the other. They may have waited in awe for the giant
sea turtle to crawl on shore, lay her eggs then watched her weary
way back to sea, leaving eggs no doubt used for tribal sustenance.
They cast about in the estuaries, seeking shellfish, combed
maritime forests for meat, nuts, berries. Their children must
have played among the dunes, strung necklaces of Yaupon.

And then?

The people came,
the aristocrats, who brought their slaves who dug the oysters, who
built the houses. The Marquis came, anchored the *La Victoire* under
the all-alone moon and in his jolly boat set out toward shore, met
slaves who rowed the crew toward their master's beam of light
in the marshes. A summer colony, later named for the Frenchman.

Was there no one else?

The keepers of light came.
First a wooden lighthouse positioned to guide the ships. The keepers
had houses near the lighthouse, firmly grounded and facing southward.
Brick by brick slaves, or so history says, built a permanent lighthouse,
the one you see before you, lit by whale oil until the new Fresnel
guided ships through the channel.

And now?

And now you come, the tourist.
Wondering what happened here under rhythms of moon and sun,
tide spilling luster in the salt marsh. The Eastern Brown Pelican
keeps watch on the ruined dock, the island once lively, lit by keepers
guiding ships in lonely vigil into a town. The island
changed by tidal accretion and sluiced, the village submerged,

or destroyed by hurricanes, the old lighthouse without
its gleaming prisms standing as though it might hold
history and drama, thick with thumbprints ancient as tides:
There is an echo of laughter—candlelight, ball gowns,
war and passing ships—it is reported, heard sometimes
among the high dunes on nights the wind is high.

Libby Bernardin
January 2015

BIBLIOGRAPHY

Auricchio, Laura. *The Marquis: Lafayette Reconsidered*. New York: Alfred A. Knopf, 2014.

Bridwell, Ronald E. *Gem of the Atlantic Seaboard*. Georgetown, SC: Georgetown Times, 1991.

———. *"That We Should Have a Port": A History of the Port of Georgetown, South Carolina, 1732–1865*. Georgetown, SC: Georgetown Times, 1982.

Brockington, Lee G. *Plantation Between the Waters: A Brief History of Hobcaw Barony*. Charleston, SC: The History Press, 2006.

Carson, Rachel, and Bob Hines. *The Edge of the Sea*. Boston: Houghton Mifflin Company, 1955.

Cote, Richard N. *Theodosia Burr Alston: Portrait of a Prodigy*. Mount Pleasant, SC: Corinthian Books, 2003.

Dusinberre, William. *Them Dark Days: Slavery in the American Rice Swamp*. Athens: University of Georgia Press, 1996.

Gottschalk, Louis. *Lafayette Comes to America*. Chicago: University of Chicago Press, 1935.

Hairr, John. *A History of South Carolina Lighthouses*. Charleston, SC: The History Press, 2014.

Horry, Brigadier General P., and Parson M.L. Weems. *The Life of General Francis Marion: A Celebrated Partisan Officer, in the Revolutionary War, Against the British and Tories in South Carolina and Georgia*. Winston-Salem, NC: John. E. Blair, 2000.

Joyner, Charles. *Down by the Riverside: A South Carolina Slave Community*. Chicago: University of Illinois Press, 1984.

Judge, Christopher. *An Archeological & Historical Study of the Georgetown Lighthouse, North Island*. Georgetown County, SC: South Carolina Department of Natural Resources, 2003.

Lachecotte, Alberta. *Georgetown Rice Plantations*. Georgetown, SC: Georgetown County Historical Society, 1993.

Pilkey, Orrin H. *Living with the South Carolina Coast*. Durham, NC: Duke University Press, 1996.

Porcher, Richard, and William Judd. *The Market Preparation of Carolina Rice: An Illustrated History of Innovations in the Lowcountry Rice Kingdom*. Columbia: University of South Carolina Press, 2014.

Quattlebaum, Paul. *The Land Called Chicora: The Carolinas Under Spanish Rule, with French Intrusions, 1520–1670*. Gainesville: University of Florida Press, 1956.

Rogers, George C., Jr. *The History of Georgetown County, South Carolina*. Georgetown, SC: Georgetown County Historical Society, 1995.

Simmons, Rick. *Defending South Carolina's Coast: The Civil War from Georgetown to Little River*. Charleston, SC: The History Press, 2009.

Talbert, Roy, Jr. *Independent Republic Quarterly* 38, nos. 1–4 (2007).

Talbert, Roy, Jr., and Meggan A. Farish. *The Journal of Peter Horry South Carolinian: Recording the New Republic, 1812–1814.* Columbia: University of South Carolina Press, 2012.

Unger, Harlow. *Lafayette.* New York: John Wiley & Sons, Inc., 2002.

INDEX

ABOUT THE AUTHOR

R obert McAlister is a retired construction engineer and manager. He and his wife, Mary, have lived in or near Georgetown, South Carolina, for much of the past sixty years. They are participants in the activities of the South Carolina Maritime Museum in Georgetown. He has written *The Lumber Boom of Coastal South Carolina*; *The Life and Times of Georgetown Sea Captain Abram Jones Slocum, 1861–1914*; and *Wooden Ships on Winyah Bay*, all published by The History Press. He has also written *Cruising Through Life*, a memoir of his family's sailing adventures.